CAMP COOKING

...made easy and kind of fun.

by Dr. Duane R. Lund

Distributed by
Adventure Publications
P.O. Box 269
Cambridge, MN 55008

Printed in the United States of America by
Lund S&R Publications
Staples, Minnesota 56479

Revised, 1984
Third Printing, 1988
Fourth Printing, 1990
Fifth Printing, 1996
Sixth Printing, 1999
Seventh Printing, 2000
Eighth Printing, 2001
Ninth Printing, 2005
Tenth Printing, 2009

You will note some blank pages throughout this book. These are for your notes.

TABLE OF CONTENTS

SO YOU'VE BEEN ELECTED CAMP COOK?

Greg Hayenga, St. Cloud, Minnesota
Photo courtesy of L.J. "Pat" Miller, Staples, Minnesota

So you've been elected camp cook?!

Well, the purpose of this book is to make your job a whole lot easier, generally more successful, and considerably less time consuming. It may even make you a hero!

Besides - hunting, fishing, and camping can be more enjoyable and more memorable if good food goes along with it.

All too often, the one who gets "stuck" with the cooking chores has less time to enjoy fishing or hunting - particularly if he takes his "election" seriously. The alternatives are to "live out of cans," prepare expensive dehydrated foods, or talk the wives (who are already not too happy that their husbands are going off by themselves to have a good time) into sending along some pre-cooked meals. Without good food, the outing just isn't going to be as much fun. Besides, successful cooking is in itself a pleasant and rewarding experience.

This book assumes the reader is totally inexperienced - except that he recognizes good food when he tastes it!

So read on! You are about to acquire a new hobby - a new interest in life - and the ability to make those hunting, fishing, and camping experiences a good deal more satisfying.

Learn to savor not only good food, but every hour you are privileged to spend out-of-doors. To help you remember and appreciate these good times, we have separated the chapters of this book with some of the experiences of *taste, touch, sound, sight,* and *smell* we recall with pleasure.

COOKING CAN BE FUN!

Greg Hayenga, St. Cloud, Minnesota
Photo courtesy of L.J."Pat" Miller, Staples, Minnesota

Because individual and regional tastes are so varied, the reader is urged to start with the "formulas" suggested and then adjust according to personal preference.

☆　☆　☆　☆　☆

To simplify and expedite your job, all measurements have been reduced to "cupfuls" and "spoonfuls" - so the only measuring devices you should need are:

(1) a common tablespoon, and
(2) a measuring cup (an average size coffee cup will do)

☆　☆　☆　☆　☆

Your camp kitchen should include the following minimum equipment:

coffee pot

toaster

iron griddle

iron kettle - with cover

iron frying pan (skillet with cover)

colander - for straining and rinsing

two or three aluminum or stainless steel sauce pans - with covers

spatula

salt and pepper shakers

large stirring spoon

large "slotted" spoon

Never wash a cast iron utensil; detergent may get into the pores. Instead, scrape the griddle and clean with paper towels. If a griddle has been washed with soap or detergent, soak in clean water. The "pores" can then be resealed by placing the griddle or pan on the stove until smoking hot. Iron kettles sometimes get so coated while cooking that they have to be washed, but try soaking in hot water and then use a "choreboy" before resorting to soap or detergent.

BEVERAGES

BEVERAGES

It is easy to toss in a few "six packs" of "whatever," but sooner or later you will probably run out and the cans do take room and are generally somewhat expensive. Besides, you'll probably find at least one of your group is a "coffee-holic;" others will be tea drinkers; and on a warm day or after a good workout the powdered "aid" drinks aren't all that bad.

COFFEE

Most cabins and camps are outfitted with a percolator coffee pot (some are even electric) and chances are most of your gang will appreciate brewed coffee over the instant varieties. There is something very special about a bubbling, gurgling coffee pot as its aroma summons the crew to breakfast or when you come into a warm cabin from out of a cold duck blind.

Here's how:

Fill the pot with whatever number of cups of cold water you want to transform into coffee. (The markings on the sides of the pot are usually for small cups.) Good coffee cannot be made without good water. Hard water, heavy in mineral content, simply will not make a good drink.

Now add one tablespoon coffee[1] (not heaping) to the basket for each cup of water. Do not rely on the markings which may be on the inside of the basket; it will probably be too strong if you do. When we take notice of the large amount of coffee the markings call for, it would be easy to suspect that the coffee companies manufacture the pots!

Be sure the water level is below the bottom of the basket.

As the pot "perks" the hot water will be generated up from the bottom of the pot through the stem which holds the basket and will flow through the ground coffee back down into the bottom of the pot.

Allow the pot to percolate three to five minutes according to taste.

---

[1]Coffee comes in several "grinds" - regular, electric percolator, and drip - to be used according to the type of coffee pot available.

For stronger or weaker coffee, vary the number of spoonfuls of ground coffee. Boiling it longer will make it stronger - but may also make it bitter. If you wish to economize, use the finest grind available. Electric coffee pots will automatically stop perking when the coffee is ready.

FOR COFFEE BOILED IN A CAN OR A POT WITHOUT A BASKET.

You don't need a fancy percolator to make good coffee; even an old tin can will do.

Bring the water to a boil, then add the coffee. (Again, about one spoonful for each cup of water you have placed in the pot.) The water will stop boiling momentarily when you add the coffee. When rapid boiling resumes, take the pot off the stove and let it settle. A little cold water added to the pot will settle the grounds more quickly.

GOURMET COFFEE

Stir an egg into the ground coffee before putting it in the pot. Add a pinch of salt. Proceed according to previous directions.

And remember, an opened can of coffee that has sat around on the shelf for months will not make a good drink!

TEA

Tea may be brewed much the same as coffee; again you will have to learn to adjust the amount of tea and time to the taste.

The instant, flow-through bags have pretty much replaced the brewing process. Simply give your tea drinkers a cup of boiling hot water and a bag and let them brew their own by leaving the bag in the cup as long as their taste dictates.

Ice Tea is traditionally made by pouring the hot tea over ice cubes. Good instant varieties are now available, however, whereby the powder is added to a glass or pitcher of iced water according to directions on the jar or package. You will find many of your tea drinkers prefer lemon and/or sugar with their drink.

POWDERED AID DRINKS

The formula is on the package. Add water, sugar, and stir vigorously.

Usually it will have a richer taste if you use *half-again* as much powder and sugar as suggested on the package.

POWDERED MILK

Follow the formula on the box - carefully. Add cold water accordingly and stir. It will taste more like "the real thing" if you let it stand - refrigerated - for a few hours or overnight before using.

RUSSIAN TEA

Prepare the tea mix before you leave home and keep it on the cabin shelf for a special hot beverage treat.

> 1 cup lemon flavored instant tea
> 2 cups tang or other orange drink mix
> 2 cups sugar (you may prefer less)
> 1 tablespoon cinnamon
> 1 tablespoon ground cloves

To serve:

Add three tablespoons of the mix to a cup of very hot water. Stir.

HOT CHOCOLATE

The envelopes or cans of the powdered variety are more convenient - particularly those which can be added to hot water instead of to milk (unless, of course, you have liquid milk in camp).

If you use milk, heat it carefully or in a double boiler; do not let milk boil or it will taste "scorched."

Here is a very handy recipe for preparing a large quantity of hot chocolate mix in advance of your trip.[1] It is also convenient in the home. It can be stored indefinitely and the kids can prepare their own drink in a very few minutes without "muss or fuss." It's also great for back-packing.

> 1 16 oz. can Nestles (or other brand) quick cocoa mix
> 1 8 oz. jar Pream (or other coffee whitener)
> 16 cups instant non-fat dry milk

Mix and stir thoroughly; store in covered container; keep dry.

To use, scoop about one-third cup of mixture into a coffee mug; fill with very hot water, and stir.

The younger members of your crew will be particularly appreciative if you don't forget the marshmallows.

Hot chocolate at bedtime will bring you good dreams of the day's hunting or fishing experiences!

[1]Mrs. Lloyd Olson, Anchorage, Alaska.

SIGHTS REMEMBERED WITH FEELING

Irregular "V's" of migrating geese, mixed with waves of high-flying mallards.

A colorful drake woodduck, resting on a log in a remote corner of a quiet ricebed.

The wild dipping and breaking of Canadian geese as they fall out of a dark autumn sky into a field of golden grain.

A partridge on a cold November day - hunkered down for warmth in a fluff of feathers along an old wilderness logging trail.

A dozen mallards on their final approach to the decoys - wings set.

A heavily antlered bull moose standing in knee deep water in a quiet bay - feeding in the early morning mist.

A shy doe - nervously leading her twin fawns through the evening shadows to the water's edge to browse and drink.

A huge northern pike - attacking a dark house decoy with noiseless violence.

The shadow of a lunker muskie following just inches behind a wobbling spoon.

The cabin kitchen table, crowded with good food - as viewed at the end of a long and successful day out-of-doors, with an appetite bordering on outright hunger.

BREAKFASTS

BREAKFASTS

FRUIT JUICES

The powdered varieties are easiest to transport and store. Follow the directions on the package or jar, but you may have to adjust to satisfy your taste. Use cold water or refrigerate. If you set the juice outside to cool, cover with foil or use a covered container - some of our tiny forest friends who also like juice may tumble in!

HOTCAKES

No outing is complete without "flapjacks" for at least one breakfast - and they really are easy to make.

A few tips to guarantee success:

- For richer, more attractive looking cakes, add one more egg beyond what is called for in the recipe on the package.
- You will have to learn the right consistency through experience, but beware of heavy batter - the cakes will be too thick and may not get done in the center. Strive for thin, light cakes - about 1/3 inch thick.
- Use a hot griddle, lightly greased. Drops of water will "dance" on the surface when it is ready.
- Make cakes about 4 to 6 inches in diameter. Never make large pancakes; they tend to be tough on the outside and raw in the center.
- Turn the cakes when bubbles appear in the batter.
- Turn the cakes only once to avoid making them tough.

PACKAGE MIX

Cakes prepared from scratch are best, but most mixes on the market today are very good and are more convenient.

Prepare the batter by following the directions on the package. Most package recipes call for the addition of milk, eggs, and a small amount of cooking oil. Powdered milk (mixed with water, of course) is an equal substitute for the liquid variety.

Just observe the tips just mentioned as you prepare the cakes.

PANCAKES FROM SCRATCH

Ingredients for enough cakes to feed four hungry campers.

> 2 cups flour
> 1-3/4 cups milk
> 2 heaping tablespoons baking powder
> 2 eggs (beat separately)
> 1/8 pound (1/2 stick) melted butter
> 3 tablespoons sugar
> 1 tablespoon (level) salt

Sift all dry ingredients into a bowl. Add eggs (already beaten) to milk and mix thoroughly. Add the milk-egg mixture to the dry ingredients - slowly - stirring as you add. Continue stirring until relatively smooth, but don't worry about small lumps. Add melted butter (or shortening) and fry on a hot griddle.

The recipe on a box of "Bisquick" also makes excellent cakes and is a very good compromise between the package mixes and cakes "from scratch."

SOURDOUGH PANCAKES[1]

Sourdough was used by the early settlers for both bread and pancakes. It would have been virtually impossible to prepare either without it under most pioneering conditions. The sourdough "starter" may be kept for long periods of time without refrigeration. Starter can be purchased in many camping supply stores or gourmet shops.

Ingredients for 16-20 cakes:

> 1 cup starter
> 1 tablespoon sugar
> 1/3 tablespoon salt
> 2 cups water
> 2 cups flour

The night before, mix the ingredients together, thoroughly (except the starter). Add the starter and mix again. Let the mixture stand overnight in a warm room. The next morning, remove a cup of the starter (for next time) and place in a jar with a tight cover. It may be stored without

[1]Courtesy Mrs. Paul Carlson, Iliamna, Alaska.

refrigeration. If the batter is too heavy you may have to stir in a little water to insure light, well-done cakes.

GOURMET CAKES

Use any of the above recipes and simply do one or more (or all) of the following:

- Add fruit, such as blueberries, to the batter.
- Add pre-fried, small pieces of bacon.
- Serve with hot syrup. Always remove the cap before heating! Place the syrup bottle in a pan of hot water. Never heat any container (can, plastic, or glass) without first removing the cover or at least puncturing the top. It will prevent an explosion!

WAFFLES

Use any of the afore mentioned pancake recipes, but make the batter a little heavier than for pancakes.

For a richer batter, substitute light cream for the milk.

Pre-heat the waffle iron until it is steaming hot. Grease the iron lightly (both surfaces) with cooking oil, butter, or margarine to prevent sticking.

Pour on the batter, not quite covering the entire surface; it will expand. Let stand about 30 seconds before closing the lid.

When the iron stops steaming it will be done. Peek cautiously to be sure!

Serve with plenty of butter or margarine and warm syrup.

FRENCH TOAST

Always a camp favorite - and a good way to use up leftover bread. In fact, fresh bread does not make as good French toast as older bread. To coat eight to ten pieces you will need:

> 4 eggs
> 1 cup of water (or milk)
> 4 heaping tablespoons pancake mix

Combine the eggs and water in a bowl with an electric mixer or hand-propelled egg beater (or a fork and lots of elbow grease). If you prefer a light coating on the toast, do not add the pancake flour; if you prefer a heavier batter, then beat the flour into the mixture. Try it both ways and with more or less flour until you get the consistency *you* like. You might also try both milk and water; however, the milk may give the toast a slightly "scorched" flavor.

Fry the toast on a hot griddle, well greased with cooking oil, butter, margarine, or bacon grease. The griddle is ready when a few drops of water "dance" on its surface. The amount of grease you will use will effect the texture of the toast. True French toast requires at least one-eighth inch of oil. Fry on both sides about four minutes each - or until brown. Add oil as the griddle dries out.

For a special touch, sprinkle on a light coat of powdered sugar and/or cinnamon and serve with hot syrup.

GOURMET FRENCH TOAST

Now if you really want to impress that crew of yours, let them see you going through the preparations for this breakfast the night before!

Four slices (will feed two)

> 3 eggs
> 3/4 cup of water (or milk)
> 1 tablespoon sugar
> 2 pinches of salt (about 1/4 tablespoon)
> 4 slices white bread, *3/4 inch* thick

When preparing for your trip, pick up a loaf of unsliced bread; most sliced breads are only about 1/2 inch thick. Homemade bread works real well.

Beat the eggs, water (or milk), sugar, and salt until thoroughly blended. Arrange the thick bread slices in a cake pan in a single layer. Pour the egg mixture over the bread, turning to coat evenly. Refrigerate, covered, *overnight*.

In the morning, fry the toast on a well-greased griddle (or in a frying pan) until brown on both sides. This takes about four minutes per side. Use cooking oil, butter or margarine.

Sprinkle lightly with powdered sugar and/or cinnamon and serve with hot syrup.

Warning! You'll be spoiled for life and will probably never again enjoy French toast in a restaurant!

EGGS

A quick and easy standby. It is really difficult to spoil fresh eggs no matter now you cook them, but you will learn that *undercooking leaves eggs watery and overcooking makes them rubbery*.

And eggs go well for lunch or as a light supper - or even just before bedtime if your crew wants a late night snack.

FRIED EGGS

Use medium to medium-high heat. Fry them in butter (with eggs, butter is better), margarine, or a light coat of bacon grease or cooking oil. If you cover the frying pan the eggs will be self-basting. When they are nearly done, a few drops of water on each yolk will "close the eyes" and the steam will help cook the eggs and make them more fluffy.

When using an open griddle, spoon the grease over the eggs two or three times while frying.

For "over easy," turn them gently - so as not to break the yolk - and leave them just long enough to sear-in the yolk. For those who like them "hard fried," just leave them a little longer, remembering that if the eggs are left too long they will get "rubbery."

Add a light dash of salt and pepper before the eggs leave the pan; let your friends add more if they wish according to individual tastes.

FRIED EGG SANDWICHES

Break the yolks about a minute after you put the eggs in the pan. Turn them over and fry until the yolks are no longer runny. Season and serve on buttered bread or toast. A light coat of mayonnaise adds flavor.

Of course, egg sandwiches are not an item for breakfast; but they go well with soup for lunch or as a late night snack.

BOILED EGGS

Place the eggs in any convenient container and cover them with water. Bring the water to a boil. Remove the pan from the stove. As a rule of thumb, soft boiled eggs take another two or three minutes to cook *after* the pan is removed from the heat. Allow ten minutes for hard boiled eggs. If you are going to eat the hard boiled eggs later, cold, leave them on the stove (just below a simmer) for fifteen minutes.

POACHED EGGS

Break the eggs onto a saucer and slide them carefully (so as not to break the yolks) into boiling water. Remove after three minutes with a large spoon (Use a slotted spoon if you have one) and serve on buttered toast. Let each season his own.

OMELETS

Omelets are fun to make and a great way to start - or end - a day out of doors. For breakfast, use two eggs per person; for supper, use three. Beat all the eggs together in a bowl until the yokes and whites are thoroughly blended. Stir in about a tablespoon of water for every two eggs. You may use milk, but the omelet will not be as fluffy.

Now comes the challenge to your creativity! You may add nothing - or a great deal. To keep your omelet moist, add a tablespoon of finely chopped onion for every four eggs. Other ingredients that go well include small pieces of pre-fried bacon, finely chopped ham, or even chopped luncheon meat. Small pieces of mushrooms or chopped or shredded cheese (cheddar or American) also go well. A tablespoon of mushrooms for every four eggs or a tablespoon of grated cheese for every two eggs is a good rule of thumb. A few pimentos will add both color and flavor. Again, individual tastes differ, so experiment!

Use a cast iron frying pan. Use medium-high heat. Coat the bottom of the pan with butter, margarine, or bacon grease. The size of the pan you use is important, because the egg mixture should be about one-third inch deep when it has been poured into the pan. By covering the pan, you will assure more uniform cooking throughout the omelet. When the omelet is well browned on the bottom (about four minutes), flip it over. If you are using a larger skillet (you can easily make as many as six portions in a medium size skillet) cut the omelet into pie-shaped, individual servings before turning. Make the cut with the edge of your spatula and turn one portion at a time. The process may seem a little "messy" because the surface of the omelet will be runny while the bottom is already firm. But it will surprise you how well it will work out - just so the bottom of the omelet is done well enough to hold together as you turn it over.

Salt and pepper lightly before the omelet leaves the pan. Each can add seasoning to suit his own taste at the table. Be sure to have the catsup bottle handy for those who want added spice.

Some prefer to fold the omelet when it is served and put some of the ingredients (pre-heated) into the fold - such as sliced mushrooms or chopped ham. A couple of spoonfuls of jam or jelly placed in the fold will also add flavor and prevent your omelet from tasting dry. Folded omelets require a smaller pan (single portion size) and a thinner omelet. In fact, omelet "purists" will insist that omelets should be prepared only as individual portions.

ISLE OF HAYLUNDGA OMELET[1]

Serves four:

> 9 eggs
> 2 tablespoons chopped onions (heaping)
> 8 slices bacon - cut into 1/2" pieces and pre-fried
> 3 tablespoons chopped cheese (American or Cheddar)
> 1 tablespoon water

Fry in light bacon grease or butter.

SCRAMBLED EGGS

Place the eggs in a bowl and stir with a fork until the yolks and whites are thoroughly blended. Add a tablespoon of water for every two eggs. Pour the mixture into a preheated, greased frying pan or onto a griddle.

[1]Named for the author's island on Lake of the Woods, Ontario.

Stir occasionally with your spatula until done. Again, cook them long enough so they are not "watery" but not so long that they get "rubbery." Season lightly and serve.

To make your eggs go farther, stir in small chunks of bread (about 1/2 inch square) before you fry the eggs.

An entirely different taste is achieved by breaking the eggs directly into the pan and stirring gently as they fry.

Any of the omelet recipes may also be scrambled; just stir occasionally with the spatula to keep the eggs in small pieces.

BREAKFAST FOODS

Somehow, it seems almost "sacrilegeous" to serve cereals on a camping trip, but they are fast and convenient. However, the cooked varieties, such as oatmeal and cream of wheat do seem more in keeping with camping traditions. Just follow the directions on the box. They may be enhanced with a dab of "real" butter and a light coat of brown sugar before pouring on the milk or "half and half."

BREAKFAST MEATS

BACON

Bacon is best broiled, but watch it carefully so that it doesn't burn.

When frying bacon, use medium heat and fry on both sides.

When frying quantities of one-half pound or more, try laying the bacon loosely in the pan. Stir the pieces around occasionally so they don't burn and they will "French-fry" in their own grease. (Save the grease; it is great for frying fish, duck fillets, etc.)

Use thick-sliced bacon when available.

Start the bacon before you fry your eggs or make pancakes.

SAUSAGE PATTIES

Breakfast pork sausage looks very much like hamburger; in fact, it really is "pork hamburger." Mold the sausage into serving size patties - about 1/3 to 1/2 inch thick. Sprinkle very lightly with salt and pepper; your butcher has already blended some seasoning into the meat.

Coat the griddle or frying pan with a light covering of cooking oil, butter, margarine, or bacon grease and fry over medium heat - on both sides. To be sure the patties are well done (and this is always important with pork), add a few drops of water and cover the pan; the steam will do the job in a couple of minutes. When using a griddle, you can check doneness by breaking off a piece with your fork to see if it is gray all the way through. Sausage patties take about the same length of time to fry as eggs.

Your local "locker" or butcher shop can make great breakfast sausage from your venison scraps. You will like it better if he adds one-third to one-half pork.

Some recipes call for the addition of fatty beef and/or beef suet instead of pork. (Frozen beef keeps longer than frozen pork) Special sausage seasoning is also added. Dark red meats, such as moose and elk, do not make as good breakfast sausage as venison.

LINK SAUSAGES

Your challenge is to make sure the sausages are well done without burning them or shrinking them too small and hard. Fry them in a greased pan over medium heat until light brown - turning them occasionally. Then add a little water (a few spoonfuls or one-fourth cup) and cover the pan. Let them steam for a couple of minutes. Start them ahead of your eggs or cakes.

Your local meat processor can make excellent breakfast link sausages from venison, caribou, moose, elk, antelope, etc. They are usually made the size of polish sausages. The difference between "polish sausages" and "breakfast sausages" is in the seasoning; breakfast sausages are much milder.

These larger sausages are best cooked in water. Fill a pan or kettle with enough water to cover the sausages; cover the container and bring the water to a good boil. Remove the pan from the heat; leave it covered; and let stand for five minutes before serving.

BREAKFAST HAM

Slice the ham a little thinner than when served as a main course and fry lightly. Do not season. All you are really doing is heating the meat. Hard frying will make it tough.

Ham and eggs with fried or hash brown potatoes make a special meal any time of day.

BREAKFAST BREADS

Toast goes better with eggs than plain bread. If you don't have a toaster, use the broiler. If your cabin does not have electricity, you can buy a metal toaster frame that sets over a gas burner or campfire and does the job quite well.

For a special breakfast - or when you have the time - bring along a package of muffin mix off your grocer's shelf and try your hand at baking. The directions will be on the package.

Breakfast breads and rolls from the grocery dairy case are equally easy, but they also take time. Don't plan on them for a morning when you are anxious to get out in the duck blind or on a deer stand before daylight.

BAKING POWDER BISCUITS

If you have the time and are in a baking mood (and this will really impress the gang), try these quick and easy biscuits; they go well with any meal but especially with a stew. In fact, the stew may be served over the biscuits.

> 2 cups flour
> 2 tablespoons (level) baking powder
> 1 tablespoon salt (level)
> 1 tablespoon sugar (level)
> 1/2 stick of butter or margarine (1/8 pound)
> 3/4 cup milk

Sift together the dry ingredients (flour, baking powder, salt, and sugar). If you don't have a "sifter," shake them together (thoroughly) in a paper bag. Using your fingers, rub soft butter or margarine into the powdered ingredients until they are uniformly coated or sticky. Add the milk and work into a soft dough. Place the dough on waxed paper or a flour covered board. Pat it out until it is uniformly about 3/4 inch thick. Cut into squares (about two inches) or cut into circles - a cookie cutter or small cover will do. Reform the scraps and make these also into biscuits.

Arrange on a greased cookie sheet or heavy foil and place in a preheated very hot oven (450°) for about 12 minutes or until well-browned. Enjoy.

BLUEBERRY MUFFINS

1 egg
1/2 tablespoon butter (melted)
2 cups flour
3-1/2 tablespoons baking powder
1 cup milk
1/2 tablespoon salt
2 tablespoons sugar
1 cup blueberries

Add the baking powder and salt to the two cups of sifted flour (sift before measuring). Now place the milk in a bowl and add the sugar. Beat the egg into the milk; melt the butter and add it to the milk-egg mixture. Sift the dry ingredients into the liquid mixture. Add the blueberries and stir gently until the ingredients are uniformly dampened. Don't worry about the lumps in the mixture.

Pour the ingredients into a muffin pan and bake in a moderate oven for about twenty-five minutes or until a toothpick thrusts easily into the muffin and they are well browned.

SMELLS TO REMEMBER

Coffee brewing on a cold morning.

Bacon frying in the pan - preferably while you are still in the bunk and someone else is preparing breakfast!

Roast duck - as you open the cabin door.

Autumn leaves burning on a warm October afternoon.

A trace of smoke from the shotgun - just after downing a partridge.

Marsh gas - stirred by your boots as you retrieve a brace of Bluewing Teal.

A meadow after a spring rain - while working a narrow trout stream as it winds its way through it.

A fresh caught string of fish - a symphony of aromas from bass, northern and walleyes.

A grove of pine trees on a hot July day.

Slabwood burning enthusiastically in the fish house stove.

LUNCHES

The members of your hunting or fishing crew may come in for lunch at different times. A good solution is to have a hearty breakfast and a big meal at night and leave a variety of snacks on the table from which each can prepare his own lunch. Besides potato chips and other packaged snacks, leave a loaf of bread and a variety of luncheon meats (in the refrigerator or camp cooler). Mustard, catsup, or mayonnaise will enhance most sandwiches.

For the more ambitious, leave a few cans of soup.

A recipe for fried egg sandwiches appears on page 21.

If you plan a meal of fish or game which are to be caught or shot on that trip - and then your luck turns bad - it pays to have on hand a "canned meal" that can be used or easily saved for a future "emergency." Cans of spaghetti and meatballs, beef stew or chow mein dinners are good examples of these emergency rations. All three dishes may be prepared quickly and easily by emptying the cans into a kettle or saucepan and heating for a few minutes (stir occasionally).

CHILI

Easy to fix - always a favorite - and it also makes a good "shore lunch." If used as a shore lunch, it will save valuable fishing or hunting time if you make it in advance and merely heat it over an open fire or on a portable gas stove.

Four generous servings:

> 1 lb. hamburger
> 1 medium onion (chopped, but not fine)
> 4 small cans tomato soup (or one large can and one small can).
> 2 cans red kidney beans (or chili beans) - #2 size

Fry the hamburger (broken into small pieces) and the chopped onion together in an iron kettle or frying pan over medium heat. Be sure the bottom is first covered with a coat of oil. When the hamburger is brown, add the tomato soup and kidney beans. Let the chili come to a boil, then turn the heat down and let simmer for fifteen minutes (or longer if you have time). Serve in bowls with crackers on the side. Luncheon meat sandwiches also go well with chili.

This recipe is for "mild" chili; if you like it "hot," add chili powder to taste.

GOURMET CHILI

Using the above basic recipe, add a small can of chopped mushrooms or mushroom pieces.

A can of tomatoes also adds a little different flavor. If the tomatoes are whole, cut them into smaller pieces before adding.

Substitute ground venison (or other wild game) for beef hamburger. Once you have used ground venison, you will never again be quite satisfied with beef chili!

BAKED BEANS (doctored from the can)

Serving for four:

1-#2-1/2 can (about 30 oz.) of pork and beans
2 pieces of thick bacon
1/2 cup brown sugar (or, 1/4 cup molasses and 1/4 cup brown sugar)
1/2 cup catsup
2 tablespoons mustard
a few pieces of green pepper
1 tablespoon chopped onion

Cut the bacon strips into half-inch pieces and fry over medium heat until light brown - not crisp. Place the pieces of bacon and a little of the grease in the bottom of a kettle. (Help the dishwashers by using the same kettle for frying the bacon as you will use for heating the beans.) Add the beans, brown sugar, catsup, mustard, onion, and green pepper. Stir and heat (medium). Bring to a slow boil, then simmer for at least fifteen m.nutes . . . the longer the better. Stir occasionally.

The key ingredients are brown sugar and catsup - so if you are short any or all of the other additives, do not hesitate to "doctor" the beans with just these two items. Molasses may be substituted for all or part of the brown sugar.

Beans are an excellent side dish with fish or meat and a good substitute for potatoes.

BEANS AND FRANKS CASSEROLE

Use the above recipe for doctored beans, but submerge chunks of wieners (about three chunks per sausage) into the beans at the outset. Figure about three wieners per serving (nine chunks per person).

This casserole may be prepared on top of the stove or in the oven. Use low heat so that the beans will not burn or stick to the container. Rubbing the inside of the kettle or casserole with butter or margarine will help prevent sticking. Cooking time is about one hour.

SAUERKRAUT AND WIENERS (or Polish Sausage)

Here's another easy one.

Four servings:

> 1 quart can or jar of sauerkraut
> 12 wieners - either whole or in chunks
> 2 tablespoons brown sugar

Empty the sauerkraut into a large sauce pan or kettle. Submerge the wieners in the kraut. Sprinkle the brown sugar lightly on top. Cook over medium heat until the mixture starts to boil. Turn the heat down and allow to simmer for twenty minutes. Since both the meat and the kraut are precooked, all you are doing is making sure both are thoroughly heated.

Polish sausage may be substituted for the wieners; two per serving if they are large.

Again, wieners or Polish Sausage made from your own wild game is always special.

SOUP AND SANDWICHES

It is a good idea to bring along a variety of canned soups on your hunting, fishing, and camping expeditions. However, dehydrated soups weigh less, occupy less space, and have the added advantage of not freezing if left in the cabin over winter.

Sometimes soups taste better when combined. For example, try adding a can of consume to two envelopes of dried vegetable soup mix. Add water according to directions but substitute the consume for an equal portion of the water you are directed to use.

Sandwiches always go well with soup. Set out the bread, mayonnaise, cheese and meats and let each make his own. Fried egg sandwiches or Denver sandwiches (an omelet between slices of toast) are also favorites.

Ring bologna, well heated in water (bring to a boil and let set, covered, for five minutes) and sliced diagonally makes a great hot sandwich. Sliced bologna may also be fried.

Your local meat processor can turn your venison and other wild game scraps into bologna, luncheon meat, summer sausage, etc.

HAMBURGERS

An old reliable - especially with the kids. Hamburgers always "hit the spot" when served with potato chips or French fries or a jar of potato salad. They may also be served with soup.

Hamburger patties, fried slowly on both sides, are best served on traditional hamburger buns. Season with salt and pepper. They can be "doctored up" by adding a little chopped onion or one-half envelope of dried onion soup mix to each pound of hamburger.

If you have time, use the charcoal broiler - with barbecue sauce for seasoning - brushed on as the hamburgers broil.

HOT DOGS

Wieners can be broiled,
Boiled, or
Roasted over an open fire for shore lunch.

They can be made extra-fancy by baking them in the oven (or over an open fire on a stick) with wrap-around strips of bread dough (from your grocer's dairy case).

For a HOT DOG SPECTACULAR, cut the wieners just over half way through - lengthwise. Place a strip of mild cheese or cheese spread in the incision. Now wrap a piece of half-fried bacon around the wiener, holding it in place with toothpicks. Place under the broiler or over charcoal until the bacon is crisp and the cheese has melted. Serve with beans and/or potato salad.

A FISH FRY FOR SHORE LUNCH

Fish never taste better than when freshly caught and served on the shores of the lake from which they were taken.

The only equipment you will need are a heavy iron skillet, a spatula, and a gas stove - unless you choose to cook over an open fire. But don't forget the utensils you will need for cooking and eating as well as dishes on which to serve the crew. It is a good idea to make a list of the utensils and ingredients required and check it before you leave camp.

For frying fish for four you will need these ingredients:

2 lbs. boneless fillets
Cracker crumbs[1] (about 1/2 lb. for every 2 lbs. of fillets)
Salt and pepper
2 eggs (bring a bowl along in which to mix the batter)
Cooking oil (or 1/2 lb. of margarine or butter)

---

[1]You may substitute flour or cornmeal - but cracker crumbs are better. A combination of flour and cracker crumbs also works well.

Prepare the cracker crumbs before you go fishing. Simply crush white soda crackers until they are fine - but not powdery.

Wash and dry the fillets (paper towels work well). If they are large, cut them into six inch lengths or less so that they can be handled more easily with a spatula or fork.

Salt and pepper the fillets on both sides.

Fill a bowl with enough water in which to dip the fillets; add the eggs and beat thoroughly - a fork will do the job.

Dip the fillets first in the egg-water batter and then in the cracker crumbs, coating both sides thoroughly. Meanwhile, add the oil to the skillet (about 1/4 inch) and place over a hot fire or flame. (If you use a gas camp stove, place the skillet on the larger burner.)

When the oil is hot (a few drops of water will crackle and pop) lay the fillets in the skillet. As the fillets brown, turn them over. Depending on the heat, the fish will take about seven or eight minutes on each side.

Serve with tartar sauce and/or lemon.

Although bread, fish and plenty of good hot coffee make an ample shore lunch; good side dishes you may want to bring along could include beans and potato chips or fried potatoes. A can of sauce will make a fine dessert.

You won't believe this until you try it, but beans (doctored according to the recipe on page 34) spread on top of fried fish fillets make a fantastic tartar sauce!

BRUNCHES

If you are up before dawn and back before noon, generous portions of any of the breakfast menus make an excellent brunch that will carry you through until supper time. A combination of fried eggs and hot cakes, for example, will satisfy the hungriest outdoorsman.

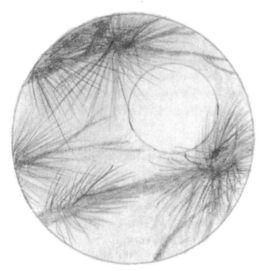

SOUNDS I LONG TO HEAR

Waves gently lapping - while catching a nap after a shore lunch.

The soft patter of rain on cabin roof and windows - while lying in a warm comfortable bed after a long, bone-aching day out of doors.

The haunting cry of a loon on a still, moonlit summer night - from across the wilderness lake.

Honking, migrating snow geese against a bright blue October sky.

The mechanical drum of partridge wings in the distance, on a warm spring night - while falling asleep.

The singing of taunt monofilament fish line as it cuts through the water followed by the whine of the reel as the fish strips line.

The whistle of distant goldeneye wings on a crisp, November morning.

The "swoosh" of bluegill wings as birds tumble into the decoys.

The distant "crack-whop" of a partner's rifle - as he scores.

The sure approach of deer to the stand, signalled by the muffled crunch of leaves and swishing alder branches.

The musical sighing and moaning of the wind in tall pines.

DINNERS

DINNERS

Diets "go out the window" (at the end of a rugged day out-of-doors) as ravenous appetites demand unbelievable amounts of food. So protect yourself by preparing larger than normal portions for the last meal of the day.

VEGETABLES

Most outdoorsmen seem to be big meat eaters. If you plan a large serving of meat as the main dish, two vegetables and perhaps a salad will be sufficient. But be sure the portions are generous.

POTATOES

BAKED

If you have the time, this is the easiest way to prepare potatoes - and always a favorite. Since large potatoes take about an hour and one-half or longer to bake through, you may have to "sneak" back to the cabin late in the afternoon and turn the oven "on" or leave directions for the first person back to camp to do so.

Choose large russet potatoes (but not enormous). Wash and scour - a choreboy works well - so that even the skins will be clean enough to be edible.

Prick a few holes in each potato - with a fork - to keep them from exploding.

For a gourmet touch, rub them with cooking oil.

Bake in a 350° oven for about an hour and a half - or until soft or easily punctured with a dinner fork.

To hasten the process, you may purchase aluminum skewers which are thrust through the potato and carry heat to the inside.

Break open and serve with butter or margarine, salt and pepper. If you bring along a carton of sour cream from your grocer's dairy case, your thoughtfulness will be appreciated.

FRIED POTATOES

Left over baked potatoes, peeled and sliced, are great fried in margarine or light grease. Otherwise, peel and boil the potatoes until almost done (test them with a fork). Then slice and fry. Use an iron skillet or griddle and fry in margarine (butter, cooking oil, and bacon grease all work well) over medium-high heat until brown. For more crisp potatoes use a little more oil and more heat. Sprinkle lightly with salt and pepper. Chopped onion adds a special flavor (about one tablespoonful per potato).

Hash Browns are prepared in the same manner, but chop the baked or boiled potatoes instead of slicing them. You may prefer to press them into patties before frying.

Raw Fried Potatoes mean just that. Peal, wash, and slice raw potatoes. Fry them over medium heat, using a little more margarine or oil than with regular fried. Allow at least a half hour to make certain the potatoes are done. A covered skillet hastens the process. For crisper fries, remove the cover the last few minutes.

French fries. Slice the potatoes into traditional sticks. Fry in a deep, preheated skillet of oil (enough to cover the fries). The oil will be hot enough when a few drops of water will crackle and pop.[1] (Watch out for flying grease!) Frozen French fries from your grocer's freezer case are much easier to prepare because it saves slicing time. If the oil is not *very* hot, the fries will be tough.

When serving fried potatoes, have the catsup bottle on the table.

BOILED POTATOES

Peel and wash eight medium size potatoes (four servings). Cut the potatoes into two or three pieces so that they will cook more quickly. Place in pan, cover with water, add a tablespoon of salt, and boil until done (a table fork will easily penetrate the potatoes and go all the way through). Do not overcook so that the potatoes become mushy or fall apart. Drain the potatoes and put them back on the heat for just a few seconds. This will dry them and make them lighter. Serve with butter or margarine or gravy.

For variety, force the boiled potatoes through a "ricer."

Small potatoes boiled whole and served with chopped parsley and melted butter are also a special treat.

Potatoes fresh from the garden in early summer have thin skins and may be boiled with their "jackets" on and served the same way. Wash them with special care before cooking.

For a special treat with fried fish, boil "new" potatoes just out of the

---

[1] When French frying, a thermometer made to fit a kettle or deep frying pan is very helpful. Try to keep the oil at about 375°.

garden in early summer and serve (mashed on the plate with a fork) with light cream (half and half) - generously sprinkled with chopped chives (grass onions). Let each person salt and pepper to taste.

POTATO PANCAKES[1]

8 "good sized" potatoes
1/4 cup milk
1/2 tablespoon baking powder
1 egg
2 level tablespoons salt
1/2 cup flour

Peel, wash, and grate the potatoes.

Place in bowl and add all other ingredients. When blended, the ingredients should be quite "runny;" this is so that the cakes will be thin.

Fry the cakes on a lightly greased griddle or frying pan over medium heat. Brown on both sides. (Turn when the cakes are sufficiently done on the bottom so that they will hold together; this can be done even though they are still quite runny in appearance.)

SWEET POTATOES

BAKED

Sweet potatoes and yams may be baked in their skins the same as other potatoes. Puncture the skin to prevent explosion. Bake in a 300° oven for about an hour and a half (longer if they are large) or until they are soft and may be easily penetrated with a table fork.

Serve with butter or margarine.

IN CASSEROLE

A special treat with little effort.

1-23 oz. can serves four if used as an "extra" vegetable; otherwise, use two cans.

Empty can into a well greased casserole or baking dish. Mash the potatoes level with a fork. Add a chunk of margarine or butter here and there.

Cover, and bake in a preheated 300° oven for about 45 minutes.

Remove the cover and spread a layer of marshmallows (small size works better) over the surface of the sweet potatoes.

Return to the oven for a few minutes (uncovered) until marshmallows have melted together and turned a light brown. If you are in a hurry, brown marshmallows by using the "over-head" broiler in your oven.

[1]Courtesy Mrs. Babe Engholm, Brainerd, Minnesota.

CORN

ON THE COB

Remove the husks and silk and break off the stem. Rinse. Place the cobs in a deep kettle and cover with water. Add a couple pinches each of salt and sugar.

Bring the water to a boil; let boil from three to five minutes (depending on the maturity of the kernels); let sit, covered, for a few minutes before serving (with butter or margarine, of course). Let each season to his own taste.

CREAM STYLE CORN

One #2 can yields three ample servings or four skimpy portions.

Empty the contents into an aluminum or stainless steel sauce pan or double broiler; add about one-third cup of milk per can and an ample chunk of butter or margarine. Pepper lightly. Let simmer over low heat (unless you use a double boiler) while you are preparing the rest of the meal. Stir regularly to prevent burning. If it should burn on the bottom, do not scrape or dislodge this corn until you have emptied the pan; it will give all of the corn a scorched taste if you do.

When using a double boiler, place the corn in the upper part and water in the lower. Let the water boil until the corn is steaming hot. The advantage of a double boiler is that the contents will never burn as long as there is water in the lower unit.

SQUAW CORN

Here's a hearty side dish that goes well in the out-of-doors.

Four servings:

> 2 cans cream style corn (#2)
> 2 tablespoons chopped green pepper
> 3 slices bacon (thick)
> 2 tablespoons chopped onion
> 2 tablespoons pimento (if you have them on hand,
> not essential to recipe)

Cut the bacon into half-inch strips and fry (not crisp). Pour off most of the grease and then add all other ingredients to the frying pan. Fry the mixture over medium heat, stirring regularly with a spatula; do not allow to stick to the bottom of the pan. When it is thoroughly heated it is ready to serve (about 12-15 minutes).

WHOLE KERNEL AND MEXICORN (contains pieces of green pepper and pimento)

Empty into a sauce pan, add a chunk of butter or margarine, season lightly with salt and pepper, and heat until steaming (need not boil).

ROASTING EARS[1]

Soak the ears of corn (husks and all) in water for at least 5 minutes. Wrap in foil and place in the embers of your camp fire (or use your charcoal grill). Remove after an hour. Strip away the husks and silk (use hot pads or "mits"), serve with salt and butter.

If you use the charcoal grill, you need not wrap the corn in foil. Just place them on the grill and turn every few minutes until the outside husks are singed.

COMPLETE DINNER PREPARED IN THE EMBERS OF YOUR CAMPFIRE (fish, corn, and potatoes)

Prepare roasting ears as above.

Select large potatoes for baking; puncture once or twice to prevent exploding; wrap in foil.

Select enough fish for your crew (crappies and sunfish work well because they are a little easier to get ready). Scale the fish and remove gills and entrails; you may also remove the head if that makes you squeamish.

Now there is one "minor" ingredient we haven't told you about which is really critical to the whole operation - you need some clay! If you are camping near a stream you should have no trouble locating some.

Wrap the fish in foil (to keep it clean) and encase the entire fish in clay (you will probably have to moisten the soil and to make it workable).

Place the fish, corn, and potatoes in the coals of your campfire and go back to fishing for an hour.

Break open the hardened clay and unwrap the vegetables. Serve with salt and pepper and butter or margarine for the corn and potatoes.

It's a little more work than you'll want to go through regularly, but you will really impress your crew with your knowledge of "survival" cooking.

Fish fillets may be substituted for the whole fish. Use the recipe on page 54 "filets baked in foil." Twenty minutes over the coals is all it will take.

[1]Courtesy Vern Seipkes, Staples, Minnesota.

CANNED OR FROZEN VEGETABLES

PEAS, ASPARAGUS, MIXED VEGETABLES, CARROTS, ETC.

The average size can (#2) and most packaged frozen vegetables contain three generous servings or four small servings.

Empty the canned or frozen vegetables into a sauce pan, add a generous pat of butter or margarine (about two tablespoonfuls), season lightly with salt and pepper, and heat until steaming hot (need not boil).

Some frozen vegetables are prepared simply by emersing the sealed plastic envelope in which they come into boiling water for the time specified on the package.

FRESH VEGETABLES

The preparation of fresh vegetables usually takes more time away from hunting or fishing, but if some well-meaning soul brings along some vegetables "fresh out of his garden," you really have little choice but to prepare them!

TOMATOES

Just slice them and serve (let each add salt or sugar as he desires). Tomato wedges are also great in a salad. Bacon, lettuce and tomato sandwiches are a favorite for lunch.

LEAF LETTUCE

Great in sandwiches.

CABBAGE

Coleslaw is an excellent salad replacement. See page 89.

Boiled Cabbage is another possibility. Very few people are neutral about boiled cabbage; either they love or detest it. But it is easy to prepare.

Cut the cabbage into wedges. Place them in a pan of boiling, salted water (a tablespoonful will do unless you are preparing more than four servings) for twenty to thirty minutes or until soft. Boiled cabbage makes a good side dish with ham or a roast.

CARROTS (and other vegetables prepared with a roast)

First of all, vegetables such as carrots and rutabagas may be washed and scraped and *served raw* or with a *dip*.

Carrots and other vegetables also go well *cooked* with a roast. Season them (salt and pepper) and add to the roaster or kettle. Just lay them along side the meat.

Cabbage wedges may also be prepared in this manner. Also, whole, peeled onions will not only taste good when prepared with a roast but will add flavor to the meat and the other vegetables.

Since vegetables will not take as long to cook as the meat, *add them to the pot or roaster the last 40 minutes.*

Carrots may also be *fried* in oil and brown sugar over low heat - turning them occasionally to prevent burning. The brown sugar will give them a candied effect.

ASPARAGUS

Wash thoroughly. Cut into one-inch pieces; save the tips.

Drop the pieces into boiling water to which a pinch of salt has been added.

After ten minutes, add the tips and let boil an additional ten minutes. Drain the asparagus and season lightly with salt and pepper.

Pour melted butter (or margarine) over the asparagus. Melt the butter over very low heat (so that it will not burn) or in a double boiler.

Plan about 1/2 to 2/3 cup of asparagus per serving.

PEAS

Strip the peas out of the pods, wash peas, then boil in salted water (more of a simmer) until tender - about ten minutes. Drain the peas and serve with melted butter (or margarine) poured over them. You may wish to save some of the liquid in which they were cooked so that you have about half water and half butter.

Plan about 1/2 to 2/3 cup of peas per serving.

CREAMED VEGETABLES

Peas, asparagus, or carrots all go well with an old fashioned cream sauce.

Four servings: Heat one-half pint of cream over very low heat (so that it will not scorch) or in a double boiler. When it is steaming hot - but not boiling - add four tablespoons of butter or margarine. After butter melts pour liquid over the drained, hot cooked vegetables and serve.

White Sauce

If you do not have cream or wish to avoid so many calories, use this basic white sauce recipe:

2 tablespoons butter
2 tablespoons flour
1 cup milk
a little salt and pepper

Melt the butter - carefully, without burning - in a sauce pan or double boiler. Add the flour and continue to cook for three minutes, stirring continuously.

Remove pan from the heat and slowly stir in the cup of milk.

Return the pan to the stove and bring to a boil, stirring all the while.

Place mixture in a double boiler, add salt and pepper, and cook until the sauce thickens.

Beat with an egg beater.

SQUASH

A great addition to any dinner after a day of hunting.

Cut the squash into serving size portions. Clean out the seeds. Sprinkle with salt and pepper and/or cinnamon. Place as large a chunk of butter or margarine in the cavity of the squash as it will hold without running over into your oven when it melts.

Bake in a 325° oven for an hour - or a little longer if the pieces are large. It will be done when the skin is soft and a table fork easily penetrates the meat.

BAKED BEANS

See page 34.

IT FEELS SO GOOD

The cool lake breeze - while trolling for walleyes at the end of a hot summer day.

Snow in the face - as a flock of "bills" wheel into the decoys.

A nap on a "soft" rock after a hearty shore lunch.

A throbbing rod as a lake trout steals line.

Solid resistance - when you set the hook into a walleye by handline - while ice fishing.

The comfortable weight of two rooster pheasants in the back of your hunting coat as you walk back to the car.

Taking your boots off - after a long day's hunt.

Your partner's handshake - after you got the big one.

A dry, goosedown sleeping bag - in a cold, damp tent.

A wool scarf - tucked around your neck and across your chest as you close the fish house door and start for home.

Bruce Lund, stretched out on a soft rock after a shore lunch.

FISH

Nothing is more appropriate on a fishing trip than at least one meal from your catch. After all - all fish taste best freshly caught.

CARE OF FISH

The eating quality of fish starts to deteriorate from the moment the fish dies. (in contrast to many meats which improve with aging) That is why it is so important to keep fish alive or place them on ice as they are caught. Never leave dead fish on the stringer or in the live box after you come in - clean them immediately and get them on ice or under refrigeration. If you have reason to believe fish will not stay alive on the stringer, you are better off bringing along a "cooler" with a day's supply of ice. Throw the fish in the ice chest as they are caught.

If you intend to keep your fish for more than a couple of days before eating, freeze them (wrap tightly). If you intend to keep them longer than a month, freeze them in water - making certain no part of the fillet is exposed to air.

The more "oily" fish, such as trout and whitefish, keep less well. Either will keep fairly well, however, for relatively short periods of time (up to a few months) if "gilled," "gutted," and frozen whole - wrap tightly in foil.

"Glazing" also helps. Dip a whole fish or fillet in a pan of ice water (use water with ice chunks in it so that it is close to freezing temperature as possible) and then place it in your freezer until ice forms. Do this three or four times until a heavy protective glaze is built up.

FRIED FILLETS

This simple recipe is just about the best we have found for any "good eating" fillet. This includes walleye, northern pike, bass (from clear, northern waters), trout, sunfish, crappies, perch, eelpout, etc. Panfish may be filleted or fried whole.

You may roll your fillets in corn meal, flour, bread crumbs, dry cereal crumbs, or special preparations off your grocer's shelf - BUT *cracker crumbs are best.* Cracker crumbs do not detract from the flavor nor are they flavorless; they have just enough saltiness to enhance the taste.

Wash and dry the fillets (paper towels work well). If the fish are large, cut the fillets into pieces about six inches long or less so that they can be easily handled in the pan. If the fish is enormous, cut cross-section steaks about one-half to three-fourths of an inch thick.

Prepare the crumbs from ordinary soda crackers. Crush them fine - but not powdery. A rolling pin is ideal for this job but if you haven't one in camp, a can or jar will do. One-fourth pound of crackers will make enough crumbs for at least one pound of fillets. Place the crumbs in a bowl.

Beat an egg into a cup of water. For more than one pound of fillets, use more eggs and more water (about one egg and one cup per pound).

Preheat the griddle or frying pan over a medium-hot stove (more hot than medium). Add a generous covering of cooking oil (or butter, margarine, or bacon grease) - about 1/4 inch. Add oil as it disappears. A couple of drops of water will spit and spatter when the griddle is ready.

Season both sides of the fillets with salt and pepper. You can be fairly generous with the seasoning because much of it will wash off in the next step, and that is: dip the fillets in the egg and milk mixture. Now dip the fillets in the cracker crumbs, making sure both sides are well covered. Lay the fillets in the preheated frying pan or on the hot griddle.

Fish will cook quickly; the fillets will be done when both sides are a deep brown - about seven or eight minutes on a side (depending on the heat).

When preparing large quantities of fish, fried fillets may be kept warm in the oven until all the fillets are ready. Fry the thick fillets first. Store them in a low oven (200°).

If you are using a frying pan, you can make sure your thick fillets are fully done by adding a couple of spoons of water and covering the pan for a minute or two. This process tends to take away the crispness, so continue to fry fish a couple of minutes on each side after you remove the cover.

In summary, for 2 lbs. of fillets you will need:

> one-third lb. cracker crumbs
> cooking oil or 1/2 lb. butter or margarine
> salt and pepper
> 2 eggs stirred into 2 cups of water

Serve your fried fish with tartar sauce and/or lemon wedges.
A meal fit for a king - or an outdoorsman!

DEEP FRIED FILLETS - IN BATTER

Fillets coated with a flour-egg batter and deep fried are very good and make an excellent change of pace.

Pour a third of a cup of beer[1] into a bowl and let sit overnight or until "flat." (Milk or water may be substituted for the beer)

Add the beer and a tablespoon of cooking oil to two cups of white flour. Mix. Beat the whites of three eggs until stiff and work them into the batter.

Dip the fillets into the batter and deep-fry in hot cooking oil (about 375°) until golden brown. The batter tends to insulate the fish so make sure they are well done before serving.

(For an extra crispiness, fold in a cup of wheaties or other dry cereal as the final step in preparing the batter[2])

DEEP FRIED FILLETS - PANCAKE BATTER[3]

Using a package pancake mix, prepare the batter exactly as you would for making pancakes (but not too heavy). Dip the fillets - without seasoning - and deep fry at 375°.

DEEP FRIED FISH AND TATERS[4]

Here is a proven favorite that makes it possible to prepare your fish and potatoes in the same kettle - making it easier to cook a meal on that small camp stove. But it will taste so good you'll find yourself preparing "fish and taters" at home - the same way.

For the batter, combine the following ingredients, mix thoroughly:

　　1 beaten egg
　　1/2 cup milk
　　3/4 cup flour
　　dash of salt
　　1 tablespoon melted butter or margarine

Preheat two quarts of cooking oil in a deep iron skillet or kettle to 375°. Slice potatoes 3/8" thick (skins included if you wish). Dip the seasoned fish fillets in batter and fry in the oil for about 30 seconds or until slightly brown before adding the potatoes. If the fillets are thick, remove the potato slices before the fish is done to prevent overcooking. Turn the fillets and potatoes frequently to insure uniform cooking. If oil retains 375° temperature and the fillets are not too thick, fish and "chips" should be done in 7-9 minutes cooking time. Serve with another vegetable and toast.

It is important that the oil be just the right temperature; therefore, you are strongly urged to bring along a thermometer (the kind that fits over the edge of the pan or kettle).

[1]If you are a "tea-totaller' don't worry about alcoholic content; it will evaporate in the frying process.

[2]Courtesy Neil Krough, Staples, Minnesota.

[3]Courtesy Earl Mergens, Staples, Minnesota

[4]Courtesy Jim Vogel, Staples, Minnesota.

BROILED FILLETS

A great alternative to frying - especially for those who are on grease-free diets. Any variety of fish may be prepared in this way, but whitefish, walleyes, and northerns are particularly tasty when broiled.

Wash and dry the fish; lightly season each fillet with salt and pepper.

Lay the fillets on a sheet of foil (to keep your oven clean).

Lay a piece of bacon on and under each fillet (cheap, fat bacon is best).

Place the fillets under the broiler for about ten minutes or less on each side. Be careful when you turn the fillets; they are very delicate. Place the bacon that was on the bottom on top of the fillet, and vice versa. The purpose of the bacon is to keep the fillets from drying out and from sticking to the foil. If you have no bacon on hand, baste with cooking oil, margarine, or whatever.

Serve with tartar sauce and/or lemon. It may remind you of lobster - but it is more tender.

FILLETS BAKED IN FOIL

Wash, dry and season the fillets.

Lay each fillet on a separate foil sheet.

On each fillet place a generous pat of margarine or butter, a thick slice of onion, and a ring of green pepper.

Fold the foil over the fillet and seal.

Place the package in a preheated 300° oven for twenty minutes. (Thick fillets take a little longer)

Serve with tartar sauce and/or lemon. You will enjoy a new taste experience that you will want to try again and again. You may also prepare fish in this manner for shore lunch - just bake them over coals.

BAKED FISH

Not all fish are good baked. Even walleye and bass are only fair. But Northern pike, muskies, and whitefish are just great. The bigger the fish the better. Whitefish should weigh at least three pounds; northerns or muskies at least five.

Preparing the fish: Scale and gut the fish; remove the head, tail, and all fins. Wash and dry the fish, inside and out.

Score the back of the fish with cross-section cuts about three inches apart - down to the backbone.

Salt and pepper, inside and out and in the cuts.

Preparing the stuffing

1 cup raisins
1/4 lb. butter (added to one cup hot water)

2 cups croutons or dry bread crumbs
1 large onion, chopped but not too fine.
salt and pepper
1 cup chopped bologna (or wieners or polish sausage or luncheon meat)

Place the croutons, raisins, meat, and onions in a bowl. Salt and pepper lightly while stirring the ingredients together.

Add and stir in the butter-hot water mixture just before stuffing the fish.

Lay a sheet of foil on the bottom of the roaster.

Stuff the fish (loosely) and place upright on the sheet of foil. Fold the foil up along both sides of the fish - do not cover the back. The foil will hold in the stuffing. If your fish is too long for the roaster, you may cut it in two and bake the two sections side by side.

Left over stuffing or additional stuffing may be baked in a foil package along side the fish or even outside the roaster.

Place a strip of bacon and a slice of onion, alternately, over each score (or cut).

Cover the roaster and place in a preheated, 300° oven. After one hour, remove cover and continue to bake until the meat becomes flaky and separates from the backbone (as viewed from the end of the fish). This should take about another half-hour, depending on the size of the fish.

Transfer the baked fish to a platter. Cut through the backbone at each score mark, separating the fish into serving-size portions. The stuffing may be lifted out with each portion as it is served.

Serve with tartar sauce and/or lemon.

FISH PATTIES[1]

Five pounds of fish fillets - diced (boneless). Walleye is probably the best but the recipe also works well with bass, northerns, crappies, etc.

2 eggs
1 cup pancake flour or bisquick
1/2 medium onion, chopped very fine
1/4 medium green pepper, chopped fine
3/4 cup milk

Dice the fish into pieces between 1/4 and 1/2 inch "square."

Beat the eggs, then stir them together with the other ingredients in a bowl. The mixture should have the consistency of potato salad. If it is too "runny," add flour; if it is too stiff, add milk.

Preheat the griddle or frying pan at 325°. Coat liberally with peanut oil (or other cooking oil) and a large pat of margarine (to help in the browning process).

[1]Courtesy Neil Krough, Staples, Minnesota.

Spoon the mixture onto the griddle into patties about 3" in diameter and no more than one-half inch thick. Fry on both sides until golden brown. Serve with beans and fried potatoes.

These patties are really a special treat and they may even be enjoyed cold.

POACHED FISH[1]

Here is a very different and exciting way to prepare firm and oily fish such as trout, whitefish, cod, or eelpout:

Fillet the fish, remove skin, and cut into serving-size pieces about six inches long. (The size doesn't really matter; you just want the pieces small enough to handle easily in the container you use for poaching.)

Fill a kettle about two-thirds full with *cold* water. Salt heavily (about one tablespoon per quart). Place the pieces of fish in the *cold* water.

Add two or three bay leaves or any other spices you prefer, such as whole black pepper or whole allspice. Add two tablespoons of vinegar - this helps kill house odors.

Bring to a boil - gradually. When the water has attained a "rolling boil," cut the heat back so that the water just simmers. Allow the kettle to simmer for fifteen minutes or until the fish can be flaked with a fork. Be careful not to overcook; this will make the fish tough.

Remove the poached fish and place on a platter; drain. Flake the fillets with a fork into fairly large pieces (bite-size). Season with salt and pepper and brush the surface of each piece with melted butter.

The fish is now ready for serving, or - you may try stirring the fish, seasoning, and butter together, or instead of brushing the butter on the fish, serve melted butter on the side in a custard bowl or small dish and let your guests dip the fish as you would dip lobster.

SMELT INTO SARDINES[2]

The smelters biggest problem is bringing home more smelt than he can really use or even give away. Right? Well, here's a great way to use and preserve these little fish - providing you like sardines.

> 2 tablespoons cooking oil
> 3 tablespoons vinegar
> 1 tablespoon salt (rounded)
> 1 pint smelt - cleaned

Prepare in a pressure cooker at 10 lb. pressure for 80 minutes. Incidentally, smelt aren't bad pickled either.

---

[1]Courtesy Ed Morey, Motley, Minnesota.
[2]Courtesy Mrs. Jerry Hayenga, St. Cloud, Minnesota.

EELPOUT HORS D' OEUVRES (mock scallops)[1]

Eelpout (freshwater cousins of the codfish) are actually very good filleted and fried. But because the meat is firmer than walleyes and northerns, they lend themselves very well to this recipe and will remind you of scallops.

Cut the eelpout fillets into bite-size pieces - about the size of scallops.
Season with salt and pepper.
Dip in water-egg batter (1 egg to a cup of water).
Roll in cracker crumbs.
Fry in about 1/4 inch oil, turning until brown on all sides.[2] The crisper the better - but not burned. Serve hot.

Now if you can forget what the fish looks like, get ready to enjoy a real delicacy!

TARTAR SAUCE

> 1 cup mayonnaise or salad dressing
> 1/4 cup sweet pickle relish
> 1 tablespoon chopped onion (fine)

Stir the pickle relish and chopped onion into the mayonnaise. Leftover tartar sauce may be kept under refrigeration in a covered container.

FIVE WAYS TO PREPARE NORTHERN PIKE
(and lick those bones!)

Everyone will agree that northern pike are among the fightingest fish that swim in fresh waters. Almost everyone will agree that the flavor of northerns is excellent - but, oh, those bones!

There are at least five ways to beat the bones:

(1) baking (which softens and separates the meat from the bones).
(2) making "salmon" of the northern (which softens, separates, and dissolves the bones),
(3) grinding (which makes them undetectable),
(4) pickling (which dissolves the bones), or - best of all -
(5) simply debone the fillets and fry them!

FRIED NORTHERN FILLETS

Yes, you can de-bone northern fillets - completely! Here's how:
First, fillet the northern the same as you would a walleye; this eliminates the backbone. Note the slight rise or hump that runs the length of the inside of the fillet; this houses those unmanagable "Y"

---

[1]Courtesy Bruce Hayenga, Staples, Minnesota.
[2]You may also use a heavier batter and deep fry them.

bones. Remove these "Y" bones by making an inverted "V" cut the length of the fillet (but not all the way through). You do this by making an angle cut on each side of the "hump" thus:

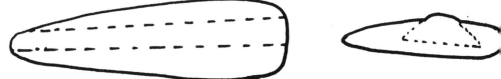

After making the "V" cuts, the entire strip can be easily removed with your fillet knife - starting at the large end of the fillet and lifting out the wedge of fish and bones as you cut.

The larger the fish, the easier it is to de-bone it.

With small northerns, about all you can do is cut off the tail piece (about 25% of the length of the fillet) which does not have a bone problem, and then make the "V" cuts all the way through, throwing away the strip of bones and fish. This will leave you with the tail piece and the two strip fillets, which, when fried, will look like commercial fish sticks - but taste much better.

Fry the fillets according to the recipe on page 51.

GROUND NORTHERN

A real taste delight for fish lovers: a crisp-fried, hamburger size fish patty served on a bun and garnished with tartar sauce, lettuce leaf, and a slice of tomato.

Fish hamburger is made by putting *the fillets*[1] through a meat grinder. If you have an old-fashioned hand grinder - run the fillets through twice.

Mix one egg into each pound of ground fish so that the patties may be formed more easily and will hold together better.

Fry the patties on both sides until brown - on a well-greased griddle or in a frying pan. If you like the outside of your fish-burgers crisp, try deep-fat frying; use enough oil so that the patty is about half-covered; when one side is done, turn the patty over. Be sure the oil is hot before you fry fish patties or they will absorb grease.

Leftover ground fish may be preserved by freezing.

FISH BALLS

Form the ground northern into balls about 1-1/2 inches in diameter. Season the balls with salt and pepper (this may be done before they are formed, but be sure the meat is evenly seasoned).

Make a white sauce according to the recipe on page 47.

Place the fish balls in a casserole, covering them completely with the white sauce.

[1]Fillet the northerns as you would walleyes: you need not worry about the "Y" bones.

Place casserole in a preheated, 300° oven and allow to simmer for 1-1/2 hrs.

Serve over boiled or mashed potatoes. Encourage guests to use additional seasoning - especially pepper.

NORTHERN PIKE INTO SALMON[1]

Impossible? Try it and see!

This recipe will dissolve the bones or soften them to the point where they will not be a problem. More important, the salmon-looking fish can then be used in any recipe calling for salmon or tuna fish (especially salads, casseroles, and sandwich spreads) or may be served cold as hors d' oeuvres.

For one pint:

> 2 cups of cut-up northern (bite-size) or other fish - even sucker
> 1 tablespoon cooking oil
> 1 tablespoon vinegar
> 1 tablespoon catsup
> 1/2 tablespoon salt

Combine all of the above ingredients and place in a pint jar.

Process in pressure cooker at 10 lbs. pressure for 90 minutes.

PICKLED NORTHERN[2]

If you like pickled herring, you'll love pickled northern!

Fillet the fish as you would a walleye - don't worry about the bones. Cut fish into small (herring-size) pieces. Wash.

Prepare a brine solution by adding one cup of salt (preferrably pickling salt) to four cups of water.

Cover the fish pieces with the brine solution and let stand overnight.

Step #2: wash off the pieces of fish and soak in white vinegar three to four days.

Step #3: drain, rinse, and place in jars (pint size is most convenient). Prepare a pickling solution as follows:

> To two cups of vinegar (if you like to use wine in cooking, use one cup of wine and one cup of vinegar) add -
> > one chopped onion (not fine)
> > one sliced lemon
> > 2 tablespoons mustard seed (level)
> > 1-3/4 cup sugar
> > 4 bay leaves
> > 5 whole cloves
> > 1 tablespoon peppercorns (level)
> > 5 or 6 small red peppers

[1]Courtesy Mrs. Jerry Hayenga, St. Cloud, Minnesota.

[2]Courtesy Mrs. Donald Hester, Cass Lake, Minnesota.

Bring the solution to a boil, then cool and pour over the fish.

Step #4: pour the pickling solution over the fish pieces you have already packed in the jars (fairly tightly). Cover and refrigerate at least three to four days before serving.

Five to six pounds of cleaned and cut-up northerns will yield approximately one gallon of pickled fish.

This recipe may also be used for pickling other kinds of fish such as tulibees, smelt, sunfish, crappies, etc.

BAKED NORTHERN (the 5th technique for beating those "Y" bones).

The recipe is on page 54.

And now the best fish recipe for last!

FRIED ALASKA[1]

Cut the fish fillets into strips 1½" x 2" in size. Salt, pepper, and paparika the strips and dust on all sides with pancake mix. (This can be done ahead of time but lay the strips in such a way that they do not touch each other or they will become moist. .

Mix enough white wine or cooking sherry with pancake mix to make a thin batter.

Heat one half inch of oil in a heavy skillet to 350°. Dip strips in batter and fry on both sides until brown.

This recipe is especially good with fillets from larger fish - which normally are hard to fry because they are so thick. Lake trout, fresh salmon, and walleyes are prime candidates for this technique.

[1]Courtesy Mrs. Paul Carlson, Iliamna, Alaska.

MEATS

HAM

BAKED, SLICED

Always a favorite and easy to prepare!

Ask your butcher to slice precooked ham for you - 3/4 inch thick. If you have big eaters, plan on about 3/4 pound of ham per serving. It is better to be on the safe side: after all, the leftover ham can always be used as breakfast meat, or in an omelet, or in sandwiches.

Spread the slices out in a shallow pan or baking dish. They may overlap but they will then take longer to heat.

Place in a preheated 300° oven and bake for about forty minutes. No seasoning required.

Serve with mustard.

Baked or fried potatoes and cream style corn or beans go especially well with ham.

CANNED HAMS

Frankly, are not as good. However, canned hams are convenient in that they can be brought along for an "emergency" in case you are planning on a meal of fresh fish or game and your luck turns bad. If unopened, a canned ham may be kept until the next trip (under refrigeration). Canned ham may be baked whole or sliced and prepared according to any of the ham recipes listed here.

BROILED HAM

3/4" slices of ham: about 3/4 pound to the serving.

Bar-B-Que Sauce for Ham (8 servings)

1 small can crushed pineapple
1/2 cup brown sugar
1/4 cup table mustard

Prepare the bar-b-que sauce by blending the crushed pineapple, brown sugar and mustard. You can do it with a spoon.

Lay the ham slices under the broiler in your stove or over charcoal. Spread a generous layer of sauce on the ham. After ten minutes, turn the ham end again coat with sauce. After another ten minutes, remove from heat and serve.

If either the ham or the sauce begins to burn, it is time to turn the meat or remove it from the heat.

There is no better way to prepare ham!

HAM STEAK, FRIED

Slice the precooked ham into servings about 1/2 inch thick.

Fry over medium heat in lightly greased pan or griddle. Since all you are doing is heating the ham, six or seven minutes on each side is sufficient (less time if the ham starts to scorch or burn). Overcooking will make ham tough. Use no seasoning.

WHOLE BAKED HAM

A practical and delicious standby for any trip: (precooked or canned ham)

It may be sliced for sandwiches, or
sliced and fried as breakfast meat, or
sliced thick and heated or fried as ham steak, or
baked whole. In this case, score the ham with cuts about 1/2 inch deep. Work ham bar-b-que sauce (as prepared above) into the cuts. Bake in a 300° oven about 15 minutes per pound of ham. No seasoning required.

STEAKS (Beef or Wild Game)

BROILED

Use thick cuts (3/4 inch to 1 inch)

If you are using venison or other wild game, trim away all fat.

Broil over hot coals or under the broiler in your stove. When the steak is well-browned, turn it over. The degree of doneness depends, of course, on two factors: heat and time. Because everyone has his own preference (rare, medium rare, medium well done, etc.) and because the heat will vary with the stove or grill, there is no time formula; but for a starter, try 5 minutes on a side. You will have to learn by experience and will probably end up testing with a knife until you've done a hundred or more - outside appearances of a steak are deceiving.

Just remember - the hotter the charcoal or broiler the better.

Place the orders for "well done" on first and the orders for rare on last so that the steaks will all be ready at the same time.

Serve on a hot platter.

FRIED

Use thick cuts.

With wild game, trim off fat.

Preheat the pan or griddle until almost "smoking hot" - use a light coat of oil.

Fry on both sides to the degree of "doneness" ordered by your guests. Again, until you have the experience, you will probably have to test with your knife[1] by making a small cut on one edge. Place the orders for "well done" on first and "rare" on last.

Season and serve on a hot platter. Seasoning steaks before or as you fry them tends to make them tougher.

BAKED STEAK

Bake only cheaper cuts of meat - such as round steak or tougher cuts of wild game. Save your choice, tender cuts for broiling or frying.

Use 1/2 to 3/4 inch steaks. (If wild game, trim off fat.)

Mushroom Style

Arrange the steaks in a single layer in a baking dish or oven pan. A skillet will do, providing it does not have a wood or plastic handle. Season lightly with salt and pepper.

Cover the steaks with mushroom soup.[2] One 26 oz. can of soup plus one can of water will cover two pounds of steaks. Be sure the liquid covers the meat.

Cover the pan or dish. If you do not have a cover that fits, use foil.

Place in preheated, 300° oven. Bake for two hours.

Swiss Steak (Tomato style)

2 pounds round steak (if wild game, trim away fat)
1 26 oz. can (large tomato soup)
1 can water
1 cup chopped celery
1 large sliced onion
1 small, sliced green pepper
salt and pepper

Season steaks and arrange in single layer in baking dish or pan.

Add chopped celery, sliced onion, and sliced green pepper.

Cover with soup mixture (tomato soup and equal amount of water). Be sure meat is covered by liquid.

---

[1]The sooner you learn to recognize when a steak is done properly just by looking at it, the batter. When you cut or pierce a steak, juices are lost.

[2]If you are a "mushroom lover," add a small can of mushroom pieces.

Place in preheated, 300° oven and bake for two hours.

Serve baked steaks with boiled, baked, or mashed potatoes. The liquid may be used as a gravy. A salad and another vegetable will complete the meal.

Baked Steak with Onion Soup Mix

Use cheaper cuts of beef (such as round steak) or tougher cuts of wild game. If wild game is used, trim away fat.

Use 1/2 to 3/4 inch cuts.

Lay steaks on foil. Place generous pats of margarine or butter here and there on steaks; about one quarter pound in all for 2 pounds of steak.

Sprinkle one envelope of dry onion soup mix over two pounds of steaks - evenly.

Bring the foil over the steaks and seal on top.

Place in preheated 250° oven for two hours.

Serve with potatoes, salad, and another vegetable. The onion soup mix may be poured into a bowl and mixed with an equal amount of hot water - then used as a gravy or poured over the steaks - or both.

This is an excellent way to prepare steaks that have been in your freezer several months (even a year). But first trim off any freezer "burn."

South Seas Marinated Steak [1]

Two pounds of steaks - 3/4 to 1 inch thick. If wild game is used, trim off fat.

Marinating Sauce

>1/2 cup salad oil
>2 tablespoons soy sauce
>1/4 cup sugar
>1/4 cup finely chopped onion
>1/2 tablespoon salt, 1/2 tablespoon pepper
>4 tablespoons sesame seed

Place steaks in a shallow dish or pan. Cover with marinade.

Let stand overnight[2] in refrigerator.

If the sauce does not cover the steaks, brush surface generously and then turn the steaks over in the morning.

Broil steaks over charcoal or under broiler. Baste with sauce.

A special treat; a different taste experience.

---

[1]Courtesy Mrs. Ralph Dokken, Evergreen, Colorado

[2]If you suspect the steaks may be tough, let stand 24 hours.

Tenderized Steak [Cube Steak]

Unless you are trying to economize, you probably will not be interested in buying cheaper cuts of beef - such as round steak - for your hunting or fishing expeditions, but even the more choice cuts of wild game can sometimes be tough. Here is one way to make them more "chewable" without sacrificing the flavor.

Sprinkle a liberal portion of flour over each steak and *vigorously* pound it into the meat. Ideally, you should use a mallet designed for the job, however, the butt end of your hunting knife will do the trick. Turn the steaks over and repeat.

Now fry them on a hot griddle or in a hot pan lightly coated with oil. The steaks will get done quickly - about four or five minutes to the side if they are about a half inch thick.

Tenderizing Meats

There are a number of meat tenderizing powders on the market which work quickly and do a good job, but they may change the flavor somewhat.

A better method - but more time consuming - is to marinate the meat.

> 1 cup white vinegar (or cooking wine or sherry)
> 1 cup water
> 10 whole cloves
> 6 bay leaves
> 1 tablespoon whole black peppers
> 1 large onion, chopped

Marinate steaks for at least 24 hours; up to three days for a roast. Keep under refrigeration. Turn steaks and roasts every 12 hours.

If you make more than two cups of marinade, use proportionately more spices.

If you don't have time to marinate wild game roast, rubbing with a solution of half water and half vinegar will help eliminate distracting flavors.

CHOPS

BROILED OR FRIED (pork, lamb, venison, etc.)

With wild game, trim off the fat.

Broil or fry on both sides until well browned (about 5 minutes a side). With pork always fry until well done. Pork chops are better crisp anyway! On the other hand, do not overcook wild game. Venison chops from a fawn take only 3 or 4 minutes over hot coals or under a broiler.

Season and serve on a hot platter.

BAKED CHOPS

Use thick or "double chops." With wild game, trim away the fat.

Season the chops, then brown both sides. Prepare wild rice stuffing according to the recipe on page 74.

Place the stuffing in a baking dish or roaster.

"Submerge" the chops in the dressing.

Cover and place in a preheated 300° oven for 1-1/2 hours. Be sure the chops are tender and well done - all the way through.

Serve with salad, baked potatoes, and one other vegetable.

ROASTS

(BEEF, VENISON, MOOSE, ELK, ETC.)

Good Quality or Tender Roasts - such as Rib, Tenderloin or Rump

Rub roast with salt, pepper, and garlic salt.

Place on a rack[1] in a shallow pan - fat side up (with wild game, remove fat and lay a couple of pieces of fat bacon on top).

Leave pan uncovered; do not add water.

Place in preheated medium oven (300-325°).

Allow

> 28-30 minutes per pound for rare
> 32-35 minutes per pound for medium
> 37-40 minutes per pound for well done.

It is a good idea to use a thermometer. It is easy to spoil a roast by having it either too well done or uncooked in the center.

A meat thermometer will read:

> 140° for rare
> 160° for medium
> 170° for well done

Baked potatoes, squash, and corn go well with a roast.

POT ROASTS *and other cheaper roasts, including tougher cuts of Wild Game*

Trim fat from the roast.

Rub in salt and pepper - you may also want to try garlic salt.

Heat trimmed beef fat (until it melts) in a heavy skillet or Dutch oven. (With wild game, throw away the fat and use cooking oil or bacon grease for the next step.)

---

[1]A raised metal grid placed in the bottom of the pan to keep a roast out of its own grease - a good idea but not critical.

Roll the roast in flour and brown all sides in the hot fat or cooking oil.

Add about one-half cup of water, cover tightly, and cook slowly for two and one-half to three hours (275° to 300° oven).

For a true pot roast dinner, add whole small onions, carrots, and whole, peeled small potatoes the last hour.

All Purpose Gravy Recipe

After you remove the roast, skim most of the fat from the remaining meat stock.

Using a covered pint jar for a shaker, add 1/2 cup of water and 1/4 cup of flour. Shake until well mixed. If you don't have a jar, use any small container. Place the flour in the container and add a little water. Using a spoon, make a smooth paste. Now add the balance of the water and stir until well blended - no lumps.

Remove the stock from the heat and slowly stir in the flour and water mixture. Return to the stove and simmer, meanwhile stirring constantly. When the gravy is bubbling all over in the pan, add a tablespoon of Kitchen Bouquet. Add salt and pepper; continue to stir for another five minutes. Serve.

STEW

(BEEF, VENISON, ELK, CARIBOU, MOOSE, ETC.)

A real favorite in camp and can be used as a shore lunch.

Since it takes so long to prepare a stew "from scratch," we are going to cheat a little! We will use canned beef stew as a base and a roast instead of regular stew meat. There just isn't enough meat in most canned stews to satisfy a hungry man.

Four servings: 2 cans of beef stew (24 oz. cans)
1 can mixed vegetables (#2 can)
1 large can tomato soup (26 oz. can)
1-1/2 to 2 pounds of beef or wild game roast, cut into bite-size portions. (Leftover roast makes great stew meat)

If you don't happen to have leftover roast, prepare the roast at home to save time in camp. Use a cheaper cut. Prepare according to instructions for pot roast on page 68. Medium doneness is best for stew meat.

Empty the contents of the cans of beef stew, mixed vegetables and tomato soup into an iron kettle or deep iron skillet. Stir in precooked meat chunks.

Simmer over open flame, on top of stove, or in a low oven (250°) for 40 minutes; stir occasionally.

Serve in bowls with crackers or luncheon meat sandwiches.

STEW FROM SCRATCH

If you have a crock pot in your cabin kitchen, you may place all ingredients - raw - in the pot before you leave camp in the morning and let simmer all day.

DEPRESSION STEW[1]

During the Great Depression of the 1930's this recipe was developed on the Iron Range of Minnesota. Wieners were very cheap in those days and were used as a "steak extender." Nowadays, the steak "extends the wieners!"

Four servings:

> 1 lb. round steak (beef, venison, or other wild game) - cut lean meat into one inch squares.
> 1 lb. wieners - cut into 1/2 inch slices.
> 1 cup catsup
> 1 cup water
> 1 large sliced onion
> salt and pepper
> 1/2 cup flour

Fry the onion slices over low heat in cooking oil or margarine for about 3 minutes.

Season the beef or venison squares with salt and pepper and roll in flour. Remove onions from pan and brown meat squares.

Add catsup and water (blend), precooked onion slices and wiener slices.

Simmer for one hour or until steak is tender.

You may need to add water to keep meat covered.

Serve over boiled or mashed potatoes.

Once you've tried this hearty dish you may feel the depression wasn't so tough after all!

LIVER - WITH ONIONS AND BACON

In many deer camps, fresh, fried liver with onions and bacon is tradition at the end of the first successful day of hunting. Liver is never better than when fresh, but it may be frozen for up to a month or two without losing too much in quality.

Four servings:

> 2 lb. liver, sliced thin (1/3 inch)
> 2 large onions, sliced
> 8 thick slices bacon
> 1 cup flour
> salt and pepper

[1]Courtesy Mike Matanich, Staples, Minnesota.

Wash the liver and trim away any tissue that may still be attached. Large livers from older animals may have a tough, outside "skin" which should be removed. Small livers from young animals are best.

Cut liver into fairly thin slices - about 1/3 inch thick.

Season the sliced liver and roll in flour, covering both sides.

Start the bacon while you are preparing the liver. After there is enough melted fat in the pan, add the onion slices. When the bacon is done, remove from pan.

Add the liver and fry with the onions. If onions start to burn, remove. Liver fries quickly - use medium heat. Overcooking may make it tough, so test with knife as it is frying on the second side (about 5 minutes a side).

Return bacon to pan (also onions if they have been removed) the last couple of minutes to reheat. Drain bacon on paper towel before serving.

Serve with fried potatoes and another vegetable, such as corn.

Catsup makes good additional seasoning for the liver and also goes well with crisp-fried potatoes.

SPAGHETTI[1]

Here's another camp favorite at the end of a long day out-of-doors and if you prepare the sauce before you leave home it will take only a few minutes to get ready.

Sauce:

Start the sauce first. Even if you have prepared it at home, it will take about twenty minutes or more to reheat. Use a medium flame so as not to burn; stir occasionally.

Brown 1-1/2 lb. hamburger
Add one small can tomato paste and one can water and simmer 15 minutes.
In a separate pan, brown one large onion (chopped) and 1 cup chopped celery.

Add the onion and celery to the hamburger-tomato mixture. Also add 2 cans tomato soup, 1/2 tsp. allspice, 1/2 tsp. ginger, 1 tsp. chili powder, and at least 1 tblsp. worchestershire sauce (more if you like it spicy). Simmer mixture for another 15 min. and serve over spaghetti.

Spaghetti:

Use about 14 oz. of long spaghetti (average size package) to serve four. Drop the spaghetti into three quartts of rapidly boiling water to which two tablespoons (level) of salt have been added. A little butter or cooking oil will keep the spaghetti from sticking together. Let boil for

[1]Courtesy Mrs. Don Jelenik, Staples, Minnesota.

about five minutes and then drain through a colander (a sieve like utensil made of metal or plastic). If you don't have a sieve use a cover to hold the spaghetti in the kettle and pour off all the water. Rinse the spaghetti thoroughly with hot water to prevent a "starchy" taste. Now add a chunk of butter or margarine (about 1/8 pound - half a stick) to the hot spaghetti and stir gently. Place the spaghetti and sauce in separate bowls and let each guest serve himself.

Spaghetti sauce may be purchased from your grocer. Often this is "meatless," so you may want to fry up a pound of hamburger - in small pieces until crumbly - and add this to the sauce.

DUCKS

A favorite with hunters - but not always a favorite with their families. So enjoy them on your hunting and fishing trips.

Most men who like duck can eat a whole bird each - particularly the smaller varieties such as Teal and "local" Bluebills. You might get by with a half mallard each if you serve "all the trimmings," including salad, stuffing, potatoes and gravy, another vegetable, bread or rolls, and dessert.

You will find that each of the several recipes which follow will give your ducks quite different flavors.

"Quick and Easy" Roast Duck

The first time you try this "fast roast" technique you'll be pleasantly surprised by the rich flavor and juicy meat.

Wash each bird thoroughly inside and out, being careful to remove every trace of lungs, windpipe, etc.

Season with salt and pepper, inside and out.

Stuff with quarters of apples or onions - or most any vegetable you have handy, including potatoes or carrots.

Place birds in roaster or baking dish, breast sides up. Place one or two strips of cheap, fat bacon on each breast.

Add one cup of water (more if you are preparing several birds in a large roaster).

Cover roaster and place in preheated very hot oven (450°) for 45 minutes. Uncover for final ten minutes.

Serve with potatoes, salad, another vegetable, and breads.

Roast Duck - "Easy but not so Quick"

Prepare exactly as above (Quick and Easy) but roast in a 300° oven for two hours or in a slow oven (225°) for three to four hours. Uncover the final half hour to brown birds.

This will be an entirely different flavor than you experienced with the quick, hot oven.

Ducks will be done when the drumstick can be easily "wiggled."

Gourmet Roast Duck with Wild Rice Stuffing and Honey Glaze

Prepare birds by scrubbing inside and out, being careful to trim away scraps of lung, etc.

Place in a large bowl, breasts down, and cover with cold water. Add two tablespoons salt per bird. Let stand in refrigerator overnight.

Prepare stuffing:

1 cup wild rice, washed (will make three cups cooked rice)
1-1/2 cups croutons
3/4 cup raisins
1/2 cup melted butter or margarine mixed with 1/2 cup hot water
1 large onion
1/3 pound chopped bologna or summer sausage or polish sausage or luncheon meat

Cook the wild rice according to one of the basic recipes on page 83.

Combine the croutons, raisins, onion and chopped meat. Season lightly with salt and pepper. Try to buy the pre-seasoned croutons, but if these aren't available or if you use dry bread, you may want to add a *little* sage seasoning.

Pour the melted butter-water mixture over the dressing and stir.

Take birds out of salt water, pat dry with paper towel, season with salt and pepper, inside and out.

Stuff the birds loosely (not packed). Additional stuffing may be prepared in foil; the package along side the bird. If there isn't room in the roaster, just set it in the oven by itself. When prepared separately, the stuffing need not be in as long as the birds - about an hour will do.

Place birds in roaster breast sides up. Place a strip of fat bacon over each breast.

Add about one-half inch of water in bottom of roaster.

Cover and place in preheated low oven (250°). Bake three hours or until tender. Drumstick should wiggle easily.

Remove cover last half hour. Remove bacon strips and spread coat of honey over breasts to glaze during these last 30 minutes. Orange marmalade also forms a tasty glaze, or baste with orange sauce prepared according to the recipe on page 78.

Duck Gravy

While duck is roasting, cook giblets (heart, gizzard, and liver) by simmering in water until tender - about 1 hour.

Chop giblets.

Remove ducks from roaster.

Skim off the excess fat.

Using a spatula, carefully scrape loose the particles from the bottom of the pan. Do not scrape so hard as to loosen severely burned materials.

Using a pint jar with a cover as a shaker, add 1/2 cup water and 1/4 cup flour. Shake well. If a covered jar is not available, use a bowl, add flour and a little water to make a smooth paste. Now add the rest of the water and stir until the mixture is uniform and there are no lumps.

Remove roaster from heat. Add chopped giblets. Slowly stir in the flour and water mixture. Place roaster on low heat on top of stove and allow to simmer, meanwhile stirring all the while. When the gravy is bubbling all over in the roaster, add one tablespoon of Kitchen Bouquet and salt and pepper. Continue to stir over heat for another five minutes and serve. For thicker gravy, add more flour and water mixture.

Scoop dressing from birds and place in serving bowl along with any additional stuffing you may have prepared separately. Ladle a few spoons of juices (or gravy) over the stuffing before serving.

Now serve with mashed potatoes, salad, another vegetable or two, dessert, and plenty of hot coffee - and enjoy one of the finest wild game dinners nature has to offer!

Duck, Goose, or Turkey in a Brown Paper Bag

If you find yourself without a roaster or covered baking dish in camp, just use a large, brown paper grocery bag. Once you have tried it, you may like it as well as a conventional roaster, and there is less clean-up mess.

Prepare the ducks as you would for roasting in a pan; stuff them if you wish.

The bag should be large enough so that the ducks do not touch the sides.

The bag should rest on a shallow tray or pan.

For a gourmet touch, fill an oven-proof cup or dish with consume' or onion soup and place this in the bag along side the ducks. If you are a wine buff, use a cup of your favorite cooking wine.

Close end of bag tightly - paper clips work well.

Roast for two hours.

The drippings that may work through the bag onto the tray - plus those that may be poured from the bag when roasting is done - may be used for making gravy. (See page 74)

The paper bag technique may also be used for GEESE and TURKEYS. Recommended roasting time for these larger birds is as follows:

6 to   8 pound bird - 2-1/2 to 3 hours
8 to 12 pound bird - 3 to 3-1/2 hours
12 to 16 pound bird - 3 to 3-3/4 hours
16 to 20 pound bird - 3-3/4 to 4-1/2 hours
20 to 24 pound bird - 4-1/2 to 5-1/2 hours

Duck in an Iron Kettle

If you have the time, always let ducks or geese soak in salted water overnight - under refrigeration.

Cut birds in half, lengthwise - with poultry shears or heavy knife. Clean. Season birds with salt and pepper.

Roll birds in flour and fry in heavily greased frying pan - about 1/3 inch oil - until well browned.

Place ducks in an iron kettle - anyway you can get them in - but remember, it is the breasts that you will want covered with liquid.

Fill kettle with water, covering ducks as much as possible.

For four ducks, add:

2 tablespoons allspice
2 tablespoons poultry seasoning
2 bay leaves
10 or 12 whole black peppers

Cover kettle (foil will do) and place in preheated 250° oven or over low-medium heat on top of stove. Let simmer for three hours or until birds are tender.

Serve with potatoes, salad, another vegetable and breads.

Par-boiled Ducks

Tough old ducks and less tasty species - including golden eyes and rice hens - will be made both tasty and tender by this technique. You might also try the previous recipe (ducks in an iron kettle) for these birds.

Let ducks stand in salted water overnight, breasts down (refrigerated).

Place birds in a kettle, breasts down, cover with salted water. Bring to a boil; remove after about five to ten minutes of boiling. If you have reason to believe birds are tough, leave a little longer.

Remove ducks from kettle, wash off any grease residue, salt and pepper inside and out.

Place ducks in roaster, breasts up, with a strip of fat bacon over each breast.

Place in preheated 250° oven and bake for another three hours. Remove cover last half hour to brown. Orange sauce (page 78), orange marmalade, or honey glaze may be added at this time (remove bacon).

This technique guaranteed to tenderize even the toughest old Greenhead!

FILLET OF DUCK

Fried

Cut the breasts, legs (at the thigh joint), and wings off the carcass and remove skin.

Salt and pepper each piece.

Roll in flour.

Fry over medium heat in about 1/4 inch of oil or margarine until brown on both sides and done all the way through (about 10 minutes for each side).

You will be in for a whole new "duck taste" experience and you'll like it!

Baked with Onion Soup Mix

Fillet the ducks same as above and skin.

Do *not* season.

Lay duck pieces on foil in a single layer.

Place a generous pat of butter or margarine on each piece (about 1/8 pound per bird).

Pour the dry onion soup mix over the duck pieces (one envelope for two ducks).

Fold the foil over the ducks and seal on top.

Place in preheated 300° oven, sealed side up, for an hour and 15 minutes.

The soup mix liquid may be used as a gravy. Simply pour in bowl and add an equal amount of hot water.

Ducks or geese that you have had in the freezer for a long time are ideal candidates for this recipe!

Bar-b-qued Duck

Let birds stand in salted water overnight, refrigerated.

Drain, shake dry, and season inside and out with salt and pepper.

Stuff bird with onion and/or apple sections or dressing (see pages 54 & 74).

Place in Weber Kettle (using charcoal heat) or on a spit over charcoal.

Roast until tender, basting occasionally with butter or margarine. Basting may be accomplished in a Weber Kettle by laying a strip or two of bacon (fat bacon is better) over each breast.

Because the speed of cooking depends so much on the amount of heat it is difficult to give a "rule of thumb." The Weber Kettle is much faster than an open spit and should take about an hour and a half. Open grill bar-b-queing may take two and one-half hours or longer. The "loose drumstick test" does not always work when cooking over charcoal.

This just may be the best duck you will ever eat!

Duck Sandwiches

Leftover duck (cold or warmed over) on dark bread with a light coat of mayonnaise is just about the greatest sandwich you'll ever enjoy.

Orange Sauce

Traditionally, duck is served with orange sauce. You probably won't want to bother with this in camp, but just in case you do, here's a good recipe:

> 2-1/2 tablespoons white sugar
> 1 cup brown sugar
> 1 tablespoon grated orange
> 1 cup orange juice (can be made from Tang or other powdered drink)
> 1 tablespoon cornstarch

Combine the above ingredients and thicken in sauce pan over medium-high heat; stir to prevent burning. For added zest, stir in a drop of tabasco sauce.

GEESE

Any duck recipe is appropriate for geese; it just takes considerably longer to get done - depending on the size of the bird (see schedule on page 76).

Because geese are usually fatter than ducks, you may need to pour off the accumulated grease several times while roasting.

Wild rice stuffing (page 74) or the baked fish stuffing (page 54) are both excellent with geese. Traditional sauerkraut stuffing also works well. Merely bring along a jar of kraut from your grocer's shelf. One pint will stuff two ducks or a large goose.

Taking Good Care of your Ducks and Geese

The sooner you draw your birds after you shoot them - the better (particularly in warm weather). In cold weather, the quality of your birds really shouldn't suffer in a day or two - especially if you hang your ducks or geese by their necks. After all, there are a few brave hunters who hang their birds for a week or more or until the bodies separate from the heads!

Before you freeze your birds, be sure they are completely cleaned - inside and out. Remove all traces of lungs, windpipes, pin feathers, etc.

If you think you may not eat your ducks for a couple of months or longer, freeze the birds in water. Ducks preserved in this manner may be kept for a year or even longer. But a better idea is to thaw out all your leftover birds at the start of each new hunting season and have them smoked. SMOKED DUCK is excellent cold, but even better heated.

Birds frozen even for a short time should be carefully wrapped, *removing all air.*

CHICKEN, PARTRIDGE, PHEASANT, QUAIL, RABBITS, SQUIRREL, ETC.

Frankly, if you are going to serve chicken, you can save a lot of time and bother by picking up a barrel or box of fried chicken parts in advance at the nearest drive-in restaurant! Keep the chicken refrigerated and merely reheat in the oven for about 20 minutes at 300 degrees. But since wild birds are not so readily available, here are some recipes for upland game which may also be used for chicken, rabbits, or squirrels.

Fried

Dissect the bird or animal (with game shears or a knife) into its several parts: drumsticks, thighs, wings, and two half-breasts (you may want to cut pheasant breast into four parts). Clean and dry.

Season each piece with salt and pepper.

Roll in flour.

Fry in covered pan over medium heat. Use a generous portion of cooking oil (about 1/3 inch). Turn each piece as it browns. Remove cover after fifteen minutes if you like crisp pieces. Larger pieces take longer. Usually, the meat will be done when all sides are brown, but check larger pieces with fork or knife to be sure. If you are doing several birds or animals, keep pieces warm in a "low" oven.

For rabbits and squirrels, soak in salt water overnight and fry with chopped onion in the pan.

Mushroom Casserole [birds, turtle, rabbits, and squirrel]

Dissect the bird or animals as for frying.

Salt and pepper each piece.

Roll in flour.

Brown each piece in cooking oil or margarine over medium heat.

Place in a casserole or baking dish and cover with mushroom soup.
(Add one can of water for each can of soup)

Place in preheated 300° oven for an hour and a half.

Your wild game will never be dry or tough.

There is no better way to prepare small game.

Turtle

If you can forget what he looks like, the old snapping turtle is a source of good meat which may be fried, roasted, fixed in a casserole (as above), or made into a soup or stew. Since the meat tends to be a bit stringy and on the tough side, it should be marinated overnight. Mix four parts of water to one part of vinegar and then add about one tablespoon of salt for every quart of mixture. Be sure the meat is all covered.

But first, of course, you have to clean the monster. Both the claws and the head are "lethal," and should be removed before operating. Begin by chopping off the head. Let the turtle lie for a couple of hours because the nervous system will react at least that long after the head is removed. The "dying" process can be speeded up by boiling the turtle for a half hour; this will also make it easier to clean. Now chop off the claws. The first few times the turtle will be easier to handle if you lay him on his back on a board or old table and drive a nail through each "paw."

The next step is to remove the bottom shell. Locate the soft cartilage "crack" where the upper and lower shells are joined on each side; this may be cut with a knife. Cut away any skin that holds the lower shell. After removing the lower shell, skin the legs and remove them - including the thighs. Next, remove the meat around the neck and at the base of the shell (tail end). You will have now salvaged about 90% of the meat, so the remainder may be discarded.

You may prepare turtle much as you would beef, but to be sure it is tender, use the recipes for mushroom casserole or stew or fix it in the oven as you would a pot roast.

WILD RICE DISHES

WILD RICE DISHES

For untold generations, wild rice was the most important vegetable product used by the Indians of Minnesota and Ontario. Outside of a small amount grown in California and Wisconsin, this area still has a natural monopoly on wild rice.

The early French explorers were much impressed with the grain and called it "wild oats."

Traditionally, it is harvested in canoes or narrow boats (so as to not beat down the crop) and the stalks of the plant are bent over the boat and struck with sticks to loosen the kernels. All of the grain does not ripen at one time and for this reason boats can go back into the area several times during the harvesting season (late August and early September).

Historically, the grain was dislodged from the husks by beating or trampling and then the husks were separated from the kernels by throwing the mixture into the air on a windy day and the lighter husks would be blown away. After the grain was parched by a fire it could be stored indefinitely.

Today, wild rice is being grown in increasing quantities in commercial paddies. "Non-shattering" varieties have been developed wherein the kernels nearly all ripened at the same time and the drained paddies may be machine-harvested. As a result, the price of wild rice has gone down while other foods have gone up several fold in the same period of time.

Wild rice is among the most delicious of foods and goes especially well with wild game. It helps make any meal served in camp very special!

Basic Recipe for preparing Wild Rice

> 3 cups of water
> 1 cup wild rice (washed) - makes 3 cups cooked rice
> salt and pepper
> 1/4 lb. melted butter or margarine

Season water with one tablespoon salt and bring to a boil. Add rice and lower the heat so that the water just simmers. Cook - covered - for about 45 minutes or until the kernels are well opened and the rice is tender. Do not overcook.

Pour off any water that has not been absorbed. Add pepper and a little more salt to taste; pour on the melted butter, and fluff with a fork.

Serve as a side dish or in any of the recipes which follow.

Alternate method:

> 1 cup wild rice (washed)
> 4 cups *boiling* water
> salt and pepper
> 1/4 pound melted butter or margarine

Pour four cups of boiling water over the cup of washed wild rice. Let stand uncovered 20 minutes.

Repeat three times.

Pour off any water that has not been absorbed. Add melted butter; fluff with fork as you salt and pepper to taste.

Another technique is to soak the rice in warm water about four hours.

Wild Rice with Mushrooms

> 1 cup wild rice
> 1/3 cup onions - chopped
> 1 cup sliced mushrooms (either canned or cooked from the wild)
> salt and pepper
> 1/4 pound butter or margarine

Prepare the wild rice by one of the above methods but do not add butter yet.

Gently fry the chopped onions in the butter (about three minutes or until the onions are "clear").

Add the onions and butter to the rice.

Stir in the mushrooms.

Season lightly as you fluff the rice with a fork.

Serve as a side dish.

Delicious variations of this recipe may be achieved by adding bits of fried bacon and/or chopped celery and/or green pepper. The celery should be fried along with the onions.

Wild Rice and Hamburger Hotdish[1]

1 cup wild rice (washed)	1 small green pepper, chopped
1 lb. hamburger (beef or wild game)	1 small jar pimentos
1 large onion, chopped	1 can mushroom soup
1 cup celery, chopped	1 can water

[1]Courtesy Mrs. Donald Hester, Cass Lake, Minnesota.

Prepare the rice by any recipe at the beginning of this section. (1 cup makes three cups cooked rice)

Fry the hamburger in a kettle. Use a little oil so it will not burn.

When it is about done, add the chopped onion, celery, and green pepper. Continue frying for another three or four minutes.

Add pimento, soup, and water.

Place in a buttered casserole dish.

Bake 1-1/2 hours in a 300° oven. Add water while baking to prevent dryness.

Wild Rice and Partridge [or Pheasant] Casserole

> 1 cup wild rice (washed)
> flour
> 2 partridges or 1 pheasant - deboned and cut up into pieces
> 1 large onion, chopped
> 1 green pepper, chopped
> 1 cup celery, chopped
> 1 small jar pimentos
> 1 can mushroom soup
> 1 can water
> salt and pepper

Cut all of the partridge breast from the bone; cut each half breast into two or three pieces. Pheasant half-breasts may be cut into more pieces because they are larger. Cut the legs and thighs from the carcass. With pheasants, separate the drumstick from the thigh. Season the meat, roll in flour, and brown in about 1/3 inch cooking oil.

Prepare the wild rice casserole according to the above recipe for "Wild Rice and Hamburger Hotdish" — leaving out the hamburger.

Add the partridge (or pheasant) meat to the casserole; stir in.

Bake in 300° oven for 1-1/2 hours. Add water from time to time to prevent dryness.

If you have leftovers you want to save for another meal, refrigerate. When you are ready to warm it, stir in as much water as necessary to achieve original consistency. Heat for about 1/2 hour in a 300° oven.

Alternate Ingredients

Duck meat goes very well with this recipe. Prebake the ducks until the meat is so well done it is easily picked from the bones. This may be achieved by roasting the birds in a 300° oven for about three hours in a covered pan with about an inch of water in the bottom. An alternate method is to boil the ducks but you will lose some of the flavor (which isn't a bad idea for those who don't care for the "wild taste" of ducks).

Turtle, squirrel, rabbit, or *steak* cubes (bite size) also are delicious with this recipe. Just brown the meat before adding it to the casserole.

In each case, follow the recipe above for "Wild Rice and Partridge."

Cabbage Rolls

For six -

1/2 cup wild rice (washed) - This will make 1-1/2 cups cooked rice.
1 cup onion, chopped
1 head cabbage, medium
1-1/2 pounds ground beef
1-1/2 cups tomato juice
1 tablespoon worchestershire sauce
1 cup sour cream (from the dairy case)
salt and pepper

Cook the wild rice.

Wash the cabbage. Take out the center core. Place the head in hot water until the leaves start to loosen or become limp. Carefully separate off a dozen of the larger leaves.

Mix together the hamburger, wild rice, onion, sour cream, worchestershire sauce, and season lightly.

Place about a third of a cup of the mixture on each leaf - as far as it will go. Roll up in each cabbage leaf and pin with toothpicks. Cover the bottom of the baking dish with cabbage leaves and then lay the cabbage rolls on this bed of leaves. Pour the tomato juice over the cabbage rolls and place in a 325° oven. Bake for about one hour and fifteen minutes. Remove the rolls and place on serving platter. Pour the tomato juice over the rolls. If you wish, you may thicken the juice by stirring in a little flour.

Wild Rice Stuffing

See page 74.

SALADS AND DESSERTS

SALADS

Most men can do without a salad - but salads do go especially well with steak, roast, or fish.

Salads can be a little time consuming, but they are fun to create.

Here are a few less imaginative but still tasty creations:

Lettuce and Tomato

> 1 head lettuce
> 2 medium tomatoes
> dressing or oil and vinegar

Break or tear the lettuce into bite-size chunks. (Using a knife is cheating - but go ahead) Cut the tomatoes into wedges. Gently toss the wedges with the lettuce pieces and serve with your favorite bottled dressing from the grocer's shelf - or oil and vinegar.

Now if you want to be creative, here are a few possible additions:

> croutons or tiny pieces of dry bread
> small pieces of chopped luncheon meat
> bacon crumbs
> tiny pieces of cheese

Let each guest add whatever he wishes.

Lettuce and Banana

> 1 head lettuce
> 2 bananas
> fruit salad dressing

Add sliced bananas to a bowl of lettuce pieces and serve with fruit salad dressing (available on your grocer's shelf).

Coleslaw[1]

> 1 medium or small head cabbage
> 1 medium or small onion
> 1 small green pepper (not essential)

[1]Mrs. Harriet Dent, Staples, Minnesota.

Grate and mix together all of the above ingredients.
Dressing:

>7/8 cup sugar
>1 tablespoon salt
>1 cup salad dressing
>1/2 cup tarragon vinegar

Blend all of the salad ingredients together and stir into the cabbage mixture.

The dressing may be prepared at home and brought with you to camp under refrigeration.

Cottage Cheese and Pineapple

>1 can pineapple rings
>1 carton cottage cheese
>leaf or head lettuce
>French or Russian dressing

Place lettuce leaf on the salad plate.
Add a pineapple ring.
Place a scoop of cottage cheese in the center of the ring.
Serve with French (or Russian) dressing.
As a final touch, add a cherry on top. Peach or pear halves may be substituted for pineapple.

"Old Reliable Salad Dressing"

If you forgot to bring your favorite bottled variety with you and just happen to have catsup and mayonnaise or salad dressing in camp -

Blend one-third cup of catsup into one cup of mayonnaise or salad dressing.

That's it!

And you'll like it.

DESSERTS

GRANOLA[1]

Here's a snack that will go great on the deerstand or in the duck blind. It is a quick energy builder and good for you. But if you leave it sitting around camp it will disappear in no time!

[1]Mrs. Russell Norberg, Staples, Minnesota.

Mix together the following ingredients:

8 cups whole oats
1 cup wheat germ
1/2 cup coconut
1/2 cup sesameseeds
1 cup raw sunflower seeds
1 cut nuts, dried apricots, dried apple sections, or whatever

Meanwhile, bring to a boil the following, and let boil for one minute:

1 cup honey
1/2 cup molasses
1/2 cup milk

Pour this mixture over the dry ingredients and mix well. Spread equally in two 9 x 13 pans. Bake 30 minutes at 325°, stirring every ten minutes until golden brown, but not too hard.

After removing from the oven, add a cup of raisins and store in refrigerator.

After a hearty meal, fancy desserts are neither necessary or appropriate. However, if you feel something is necessary, try -

Cookies with that after-dinner cup of coffee,

sauce from the can, - chilled,

bakery goods or baked goodies from home (your wife's are better anyway), or

serve the "lazy man's standby:" ice cream, with a selection of toppings so each can make his own sundae.

NOW -

ENJOY COOKING
and
ENJOY THE RESULTS!

BON APPETITE!

DIDN'T THAT TASTE GOOD?

Scalding hot coffee in the duck blind.

A long, cold drink from a mountain stream - while lying on your belly with your face in the water - after a hot, exhausting climb.

Crisp fillet of walleye pike on a thick slice of homemade bread, well buttered and enjoyed on the rocky shores of a clear lake after a good morning of fishing.

Breast of duck on rye - enjoyed at noon on the deer stand.

A crisp apple as you rest on a fat log - while "still hunting" for deer.

Special dishes made from wild foods you have harvested yourself, whether it be -

> blueberry pie,
>
> wild strawberry or raspberry sauce,
>
> chokecherry, pincherry, or high bush cranberry jell - served with wild game.
>
> butter-fried mushrooms,
>
> wild rice stuffing, or
>
> hazel nuts, dried on the shed roof and cracked by the fireplace.

Other Books by Duane R. Lund

About the Author

- EDUCATOR (RETIRED, SUPERINTENDENT OF SCHOOLS, STAPLES, MINNESOTA);
- HISTORIAN (PAST MEMBER OF EXECUTIVE BOARD, MINNESOTA HISTORICAL SOCIETY); Past Member of BWCA and National Wilderness Trails Advisory Committees;
- SENIOR CONSULTANT to the Blandin Foundation
- WILDLIFE ARTIST, OUTDOORSMAN.